WITH EXTREME PREJUDICE

An Investigation into Police Vigilantism in Manchester

Martin Walker

Canary Press

With Extreme Prejudice

ISBN 0 9509967 8 5

Published by Canary Press
First Edition October 1986

Typeset by Grassroots, London NW6
01-328 0318
Set in CG Times 10 on 12 points
Printed in England by Biddles, Guildford

Cover design by Andy Dark/Graphics International, London N1
01-833 2988

Martin Walker

Martin Walker was born in Manchester in1947 and trained as a graphic designer at Hornsey College of Art. This is his fifth book. Over the last ten years he has been involved in research and campaigning around prisons, policing and the criminal law; he has also investigated and written on particular criminal cases. 'State of Siege', written with Susan Miller and Jim Coulter on the policing of the 1984-85 miners' strike and 'Turn of the Screw', on the sacking, imprisonment and victimisation of miners following the strike, are both published by Canary Press.

Acknowledgements

This book was written under unusual and at times extreme pressure. For most of my time in Manchester I felt under threat, concerned that I was being followed and that phones were being tapped. Fears that the office I was working in would be burgled and my papers stolen drove me to seek secure accommodation and to keep the manuscript in a safe. In light of all these problems and given the very serious attacks that there had been on Steven and Sarah, it was particularly refreshing that so many people were eager to help with the book. However because of the conditions still prevailing in Manchester, I have decided to acknowledge people by their first names only.

Like all books, this book could not have been written without a great deal of ancillary research and editorial work, for the first, I have to thank Mary who worked with a singular commitment, despite othe responsibilities. In London Babs did extensive work on editing the manuscript and without her help and dedication the book would not have reached its final form. Sue worked on the table of the trials and uncovered important information from the transcripts.

During the writting of the book I worked in accommodation provided for me by the student union executive of UMIST and I am particularly grateful to Tim for all the work he did in this respect. The investigation into the case of Steven Shaw was and still is being carried out by a number of people besides myself and to some extent the information in this book is compound of their work as well as mine; David, Ann, Tim, Steve, Davey, Bill, and Surinda.

There are many people mentioned in the book who gave up their time to be interviewed, most obviously Steven Shaw who also researched many of the references and footnotes. Dom was always available with a clear and perceptive analysis of the events described.

While I stayed in Manchester, life was made more enjoyable by the support which I was given by many students, particularly those in Norman Road. In London, members of the Canary Press Collective gave me support, as did Andy and Paul with the graphics and photographs. I am particularly grateful to those people who, at short notice, gave their help with reading the manuscript and giving legal opinions.

Since February 1986, Steven's case has been regularly discussed by a collective of people from London and Manchester. All these people contributed in different ways to the production of the book; James, Gareth, Mike, Tony, Ann, Tony, Tim, Duncan and Olivia. A number of people read the manuscript in draft form and made suggestions, some of them have already been mentioned but I am particularly grateful to Duncan, David and Helen.

Finally, I have to thank members of Manchester City Council, Manchester University Students Union and members of the AUT at Manchester University. Although these groups all provided a great deal of support and initiative, and without them, the book could not have been produced, it goes without saying that the opinions in it are mine and not theirs. In particular I want to thank Tony, Paul, Vick and Chris.

★ ★ ★

I wish to make it clear, particularly to those police officers who were involved in the attacks upon Sarah Hollis, that she has had nothing to do with the production of this book. At no time have I sought her help and at no time have I received any communication from her offering me help. All the information about Sarah in this book is culled from statements which she gave to the police and from newspaper reports.

★ ★ ★

The story in this book is not intended to be a reflection upon *all* the police officers of the Greater Manchester Force. There must be officers in the force who are not sympathetic to threatening young female citizens with rape and stubbing cigarettes out on people's faces. However, as long as these officers remain silent, and as long as the Greater Manchester Branch of the Police Federation reacts with a sense of blind loyalty to all its officers, it is inevitable that they will be tarred with the same brush as their corrupt colleagues. This misplaced sense of loyalty to corrupt officers and those who carry out violent attacks can do nothing but worsen the view that the people of Manchester have of the police.

Author's Preface

In the early evening of March 1st 1985, a few days before the end of the miners' strike, the then Home Secretary, Leon Brittan, visited Manchester University Students Union to give a talk on 'Law and Order.' Three hundred or so students mounted a picket on the steps of their building to protest against the visit and government policies. Before escorting Brittan into the building, the police broke up the demonstration and over a period of two hours injured a number of students and arrested thirty eight others. In the year following this visit, while two antagonistic inquiries worked, from different points of view, to establish what had happened, two students, Steven Shaw and Sarah Hollis, became the victims of an anonymous and violent campaign of intimidation. This book argues the case for the students against the Greater Manchester Police, whom they believe were responsible for the harassment.

I first met Steven Shaw in October 1985. By this time, he had been burgled, harassed in the street and held in Bootle Street police station for almost five hours. The independent inquiry set up by Manchester City Council had published its report, two television programmes and a number of newspaper articles had publicised both his case and that of Sarah Hollis.

When the harassment showed no signs of ending, even after this publicity, I was approached by Manchester City Council Police Monitoring Unit for advice and help. But the problem I had was the same as theirs and of Steven's solicitor; without understanding the context or the reason for the harassment, how did we prevent it continuing? How do you protect someone against a series of anonymous attacks? Where do you begin looking for the culprits? It wasn't until February 1986 that those involved in the case concluded that the only possible protection was more publicity.

By that time, I was in Manchester helping to investigate the case. The task we had set ourselves was extremely difficult, quite different from investigating cases against named officers, within the context of a particular arrest or court case. Here we were floundering with no names and no context.

Difficult as it is to admit defeat, it looks now very much as if this case will remain unsolved. We might have to wait for real political change before we can get anywhere near the police officers who created a reign of terror for two young students. In the meantime, it is the kind of case which makes you anxious for the future; the kind of case which makes you want to scream. It is a case which mesmerises you with frustration. But none of this means that the investigation has been a waste of time. The case is a pointer to what we may expect in the future and it gives a real understanding of who the police are and the role which they play in our society.

Cases of this kind do not have the easy symmetry of their counterparts in popular fiction. In the real world, such cases present us with political rather than simply logical or legal solutions. Consequently, this book is about the politics of policing and the politics of dissent.

Both the students who found themselves victims of harassment were beaten on different occasions. Although it is possible to record and understand these attacks as social facts, as we might understand racist attacks, it is not so easy to determine either the motivation for them or the consciousness which lies behind them, in any objective way. The police of two different forces, for their part, have done next to nothing to find the assailants or uncover the conspiracy. In the light of those facts which do exist, *they* were drawn to only two conclusions, either the harassment was composed of many disjointed and unordered incidents which were unrelated to policing, or there was no truth in the allegations made by the two students. On the latter possibility many officers went further and claimed that if there was a conspiracy it was organised by the complainants themselves. By drawing upon either or both of these hypotheses the police were effectively able to ignore a series of serious crimes. All the powers and technical resources which they employ in the investigation of crimes against the powerful turned to dust when the lives of ordinary people were in danger.

A remark from one of the investigating officers throws light on the police attitude: 'We have not found the attackers because we cannot find a motive.' This remark explains a great deal about the political perspectives of detectives. The statement shows that while we might imagine that they work objectively, building a case upon clues and material facts, the work is usually governed by ideas and political will. This kind of statement was not made once during the miners' strike when the police arrested 10,000 people; it was not made after the conflicts on Broadwater Farm. Nor is it usually made in cases of murder or robbery, which most police officers believe are 'normal' activities in our present society. It is never made when a police officer is attacked, or a leading industrialist killed. In all these examples, the facts of the investigation simply go towards confirming the preconceived ideas of the detective and the force within which he works. The police officers investigating the harassment of Steven Shaw and Sarah Hollis should have known the motive, but they were apparently unwilling to acknowledge the fact that police officers commit crimes and they failed to go to work on what is now a well accepted precept that police officers who are the subject of complaint often try to conceal their offences.

While it might be possible to view social facts and material realities with some degree of objectivity, the police do not actually do this; the work of detection is heavily laden with preconceived value judgements. The understanding of motive, and more, the consideration of motive before the facts are assessed, involves value judgements based upon psychology, culture and ideology[1]. Definitions of crime and methods of detection are not based primarily upon scientific objectivity but in the first instance upon ideas of class, sexual attitudes, political philosophy and an intuitive understanding of the structures of social power.

In writing the book, I also have considered it proper to begin from a position of my ideas about class, culture and ideology. These attitudes are based upon my fourteen years of investigating the police. I have chosen to present some conclusions and some theoretical considerations, not at the end of the book, but near the beginning. In doing this, I have done exactly as the police did during their investigation; my assumptions and their assumptions are however slightly different. There is also a difference between the way in which I have written the book and the way the police investigated the case. I *have* presented the facts and they are incorporated in my theoretical assumptions. Whenever the police came across facts they ignored them or, if they were unable to ignore them, they changed or suppressed them.

Systems of objectivity are themselves based upon assumptions of the prevailing ideology. In this kind of case, the prevailing ideology tells us, and has told us countless times, inside and outside the courts, that police officers do not commit crimes; if they do their motives are often said to be completely justifiable.

If there is a hidden story in this book it is the story of realities in collision; a war of ideas and cultural languages which goes on ceaslessly surrounding the objective facts of our lives. The police in our present society are at the forefront of propagating the State's reality, and even where this confounds facts, we are expected to accept it as the only reality.

It would be hard to be objective in a book of this kind and I do not believe that the objectivity of the limited facts available could bring us any nearer a resolution to the case. At every point we find ourselves dealing with police consciousness and politics as against quantifiable facts. In this particular instance, as in the case of Hilda Murell, those who control the social reality also have complete control of the evidence.

Those who conducted the campaign of intimidation against Steve Shaw and Sarah Hollis were part of a highly organised, powerful and resourceful institution. The reason for the harassment, if we can talk of reason in this context, was the protection and defence of officers who had themselves committed offences. From the beginning we were dealing with a group of people who had a vested interest which led them to act with careful secrecy in destroying any evidence against them. In such circumstances, to talk of objectivity is to render oneself defenceless; it is to take up an unenquiring position, outside of the case.

There are no neutral positions, and the police are well aware of this. They are also aware that ordinary people desperately wish to believe that there are. Most people avoid conflict if they can, or limit it to manageable proportions. Others, by design or accident, have conflict thrust upon them; from an ordinary and quiet life, they find themselves suddenly pushed into a struggle for their very survival. Such people, if they are not to become victims, cannot afford to entertain ideas of objectivity.

This book is written for those who find themselves propelled into conflict without choice. It is written for and on behalf of those who, like Steven Shaw and his family, have found the courage to overcome objectivity and fight back. The book rarely addresses the middle ground, because objectively, the middle ground is addressed evey minute of the day, every day of the week, by the media and the ruling institutions of our society, which reduce every phenomenon to a list of facts. This 'objective' voice, which has its own inner political reality, is more than adequately represented.

The facts alone are not enough. Increasingly we have to try and understand not simply what happens, but why it happens. Our simple knowledge of the facts does not actually set our feet on the road to changing anything. In its most limited sense, this book is about changing something, changing a condition in Manchester, at least temporarily, where police officers can organise attacks upon defenceless people. We all have our defence against getting involved; the cause is too small, or the cause is to great, it disturbs our psychological safety or disrupts our physical routine. But at base, the matter is simple; if after reading this book you choose to ignore what happened to Steven Shaw and Sarah Hollis, then you acquiesce in the crimes committed against them and you help pave the way for the ultimate victimisation of us all.

CONTENTS

PART ONE

THE EMPEROR'S NEW CLOTHES

Police vigilantism is the furthest excursion which the police can make outside the constraints of the law, since vigilantism is a species of action that is no more and no less than a law unto itself.

Tom Bowden: Beyond the Limits of the Law

Our own ideology, as it must, forbids us ever to question and analyse the structure of what we hold to be true, since only thus can we maintain the fiction that we choose to believe what in fact we have no choice but to believe, short of ostracism or insanity.

Erik Erikson: Young Man Luther;
A Study in Psychoanalysis and History

INTRODUCTION

I am an honest and truthful man who puts his trust in God and fears nothing from any complaints.

James Anderton

The fish rots from the head down.

Chinese proverb

The Destruction of Jackie Berkeley

In February 1985, a trial began in Manchester which should have been recognised as an important turning point in the developing legitimation of police powers and the criminalisation of ordinary people. In fact, the three week trial passed with hardly a mention. The accused in Manchester Magistrates Court room 7, on February 13th, was Jacqueline Berkeley, a twenty year old English woman of West Indian descent. The offended party was the Greater Manchester police force. The case had been brought by the Director of Public Prosecutions.[2]

This particular trial was never a test of fact or a search for the truth. To many observers it appeared more to be an attempt by a powerful institution to destroy the identity of a young black woman. Jackie Berkeley had made a serious complaint against Greater Manchester police officers.

On April 19th, 1984, Jackie Berkeley intervened to stop a fight between two groups of young women. The police, who were already at the scene, arrested her as one of the participants. On April 24th, five days after her arrest, Jackie told a youth worker that something terrible had happened to her inside Greenheys Lane Police Station (Greenheys Lane is the new and deceptively pleasant name for Moss Side Police Station). She said that when she arrived at the police station, she was put in a single cell. While in the cell, she was beaten, racially abused and finally raped by two male officers while being held on the floor by two W.P.C's.

On April 25th after she had repeated the story to her parents and a solicitor, an official complaint was laid against the police. An internal investigation was started under the guidance of the Chief Superintendent who was the head of the Greater Manchester Police complaints department. It was carried out by another male Chief Inspector, and a female Detective Sergeant. By the time that Jackie made her complaint, there was no forensic evidence to support her claim;[3] she was forced to rely completely upon police officers to piece together the events surrounding her accusation.

Throughout the investigation, Jackie was subjected to intensive interviews and made to repeat again and again all the information which she had originally given. Despite the fact that she appeared to have a clear idea of which police officers had raped her, and that there were few officers on duty in the station that night, she was asked to attend 22 identification parades which included officers from all over the Greater Manchester area. The parades took six hours, but even so, Jackie managed to identify the two WPC's and one of the male constables whom she said were responsible.

The officers that Jackie picked out had all been present in Greenheys Lane on the night she claimed she was raped. After the parades, they and all the other officers in the station were allowed to make self recorded statements, alone, and in their own time. No officers were arrested or suspended.

The internal investigation into Jackie's complaint found no truth in her accusation, and concluded that she had acted in a manner which was 'malicious and wicked.' The case was referred to the Director of Public Prosecutions and on the advice of the Greater Manchester police she was charged with 'wasting police time.'[4] On this charge, the defendant cannot elect for trial by jury. Jackie was subsequently tried before a Stipendiary Magistrate in Manchester Magistrates Court.

The intense internal police investigation, and the harrassment which this brought to the rest of her family, on top of her original treatment inside the police station, began to destroy Jackie. She tried to commit suicide. During her appearance in court, she was depressed and unable to communicate properly. At one point the Magistrate told her; 'I'm quite sure that you speak much louder than this at home.' The media expressed concerted disbelief in her and the whole case came to rest publically upon the fact that she had not reported the alleged rape to the police immediately it had happened.

The expert witnesses who appeared on Jackie's behalf,

psychologists, rape counsellors and academics, gave evidence that her behaviour was entirely consistent with that of a young woman who had been raped. The defence established that her pants had been torn from her body.

The evidence of police officers was put under strain by defence cross examination; officers contradicted themselves and each other. In his closing speech to the magistrate, the defence counsel presented evidence which tried to establish that the culture of the police force in Manchester and other inner city areas developed and propagated certain attitudes towards women, and black people, which were quite consistent with them raping a black woman prisoner.

Jacqueline Berkeley was found guilty of wasting police time. The Magistrate expressed the view that there could not be the slightest possibility that she had been raped by police officers; he dwelt heavily upon the lapse of time between her arrest and the report which she gave to the youth worker.

What made this trial so different from the others which teem through the inner city courts is that it was not a trial over facts or even acts. What was at stake in Jacqueline Berkeley's trial was her identity; black and female. What was at stake for the State was the identity of the police force; mainly male and white. The power of the State and its agents the police is, as many working class people can testify, a physical power; it grows from the baton, the fist and the gun, the body of the human machine and its technological aids. But beyond all this, that power is the symbolic and evidential proof of the most powerful social reality.

Only the state is allowed to dispute cultural and political realities in a court of law. The counsel for Jacqueline Berkeley had an almost impossible task. Even if he had been able to prove materially that police officers had raped her, and even if following *her* trial there had been a prosecution, the proof would have to have been absolute and irrefutable to gain a conviction. Those who hold the power in the State would say, even in the face of material evidence to the contrary, that police officers are not capable of raping a woman in custody. They need have no evidence for this assertion, which is based upon their consciousness. At the centre of bourgeois State consciousness nestles the concept of the purity of the State; the integrity of the State and all its agents. This concept is counter balanced with that of the criminality of the people, their duplicity and their lack of integrity.

The prevailing culture of the State determines the individual identity of anyone who does not have a stake in the State as criminal. The greater the social distance of the individual from its institutions, the greater is the State's need to dispute their reality and their identity. The black woman comes at the farthest end of this spectrum, she is seen as dehumanised 'slag' of the most impure kind. The further away from the State insitutions the individual identity is, the greater the crimes which can be committed with impunity against that individual by the agents of the State.

The police are the physical power of the State. Gradually they move to control both the bodies and the material space of society. First they control the ragged and confused areas of property ownership, then they move to control the physical space of the streets; once they control the material and public city, they move into the domestic space of individuals in society, gaining control over indoor meetings and domestic residences. But finally, this control is not enough and after attempts to control the physical body of the individual by constraint and incarceration, they demand power over the internal body and the identity. The exercise of power has no boundaries, its ultimate objective is the control of consciousness and feeling.

It is culture, in this case police culture, which builds the ideology which supports these structures of power. A culture of the State begins in its earliest stages to separate those who have freedom from those who cannot be allowed freedom; those who have denied themselves feeling from those who wish to express feeling; those who are of productive use from those who are deemed to be of no worth. An inhuman sub-class is generated which is by its very nature uncontrollable and therefore subversive.

In the exercise of power every calumny can be acted out against those who do not adhere to the State's philosophy. They can be batoned and abused, injured and killed. Finally they can be tortured; naked power for its own sake can be exercised against them. Torture in all countries is used most especially by the police and the armed forces against those who resist the reality of the ruling institutions. The key to successful torture is the exertion of power over the *internal identity* of the individual. The most effective forms of torture damage and change the sexual or emotional identity of the individual.

The trial of Jackie Berkeley for wasting police time was a test of how powerful the reality of the police is in our society. Her conviction was an affirmation of the reality and the power granted to the police of Greater Manchester by the State; it was a green light.

The Second Coming of Oliver Cromwell

Manchester is England's second largest city, and like other large manufacturing centres it is a city going through changes. Slowly it is leaving behind the smoky darkness of the industrial revolution and edging its way into the bright new dehumanised dawn of high technology capitalism. Although this fundamental change makes itself felt most strongly in the old industrial centres, its political and economic epicentre is in the South of England. While statutes and orders are despatched from the capital, with an almost imperial disregard for their effects, the people and the local State in the old industrial centres struggle to survive. Wastelands are created by the change from labour intensive industry to the more diffuse high technology production. Communities are destroyed or pauperised and groups on the economic fringe struggle, without proper work, to make ends meet.

Change never happens evenly. The difficulties implicit in imposing a new economic order, together with the social consciousness of the past, send parts of the society racing away; others are left stuck in eddying and stagnant backwaters. In the nineteenth century Manchester was the centre of the industrial revolution, the engine of Britain's wealth built upon cotton and slavery. Now the new glitters unevenly in the dark brick city like pyrites in coal shale. Everywhere there is evidence of the change. To those who know Manchester, three symbols of the transformation might come to mind; the city's sewers, it's Royal Exchange Theatre and its Police Chief.

The sewers grew with the industrial revolution and a massive programme of civic amenities in the last century. They exemplified the progressive aspect of the new industrial middle class. Now, their old castings rust and disintegrate. The City Council, deprived of funds for a similar but more modern programme of civic building, has matched and patched as it can. Gaping holes appear with regularity in the roads and pavements; some big enough to swallow a bus. The architecture of the last industrial revolution imposes its price upon the cost cut conditions of the next.

The Royal Exchange Theatre has been built within the old cotton exchange. As in the docklands of London and Manchester, the architecture of a past age of commerce has been usurped for the pursuit of present day leisure. While the exchange towers around it, the theatre, like a lost lunar module, sits with insecure pretentions in the middle of the stone floor. Where once wealth was bought and sold, where dynasties and power brokers duelled and fought, a trickle of the nouveaux riches now step lightly in and out. The theatre itself, all plastic and aluminium pipes, glass and wire string, is a monument to the the new technology; a new kernel within an old husk.

James Anderton has been the Chief Constable of Greater Manchester for ten years. Though a bête noir of the political left, he is not wholly a creature of the new State, a man of steel and glass, nor is he simply a paternalist of the last more liberal century. Neither entirely fitted for the new world, nor too out-of-step with the old to be discarded. Anderton personally, and his force corporately, represent very clearly the contradictions between the industrial revolution and the brave new world.

In a modern society whose god is the State, Anderton espouses a peculiarly individualistic approach to the religious tenets of the last century. He is a Mancunian Ian Paisley, a city and county chauvinist rather than a State nationalist. His views are infused with the hard protestant morality which built the nineteenth century. A Methodist lay preacher who believes in reincarnation, he once hinted that he could be the reincarnation of Oliver Cromwell[5].

In 1977, the Manchester police force was one of the first to raid record shops and seize displays of the Sex Pistols album 'Never Mind the Bollocks.' In the late seventies his officers conducted a ceaseless war against local newsagents who stocked 'girlie' magazines. He has in the past advocated corporal punishment for young people on the grounds that it never did him any harm. His old fashioned religious tenets however, sometimes drive him, Christ-like, to criticise the emphasis which the class he represents places upon money and profit:

> So many things effect crime and public disorder; the relax-

> ing of self control by eroding discipline; *the cynical promotion of envy for the sake of profit,* and the ruthless denigration of those morals upon which *valid* social progress is built.[6] (author's italics)

This puritanism from an earlier age coexists with an easy acceptance of moves towards a totalitarian State. Greater Manchester police were the first to be issued publicly with sub-machine guns[7], and the first to publicly acknowledge the carrying of hand guns on normal duty. He has at different times proposed the fingerprinting of the whole population and the internment of subversives in camps.

For years James Anderton has fought a war of impatience, intolerance and scepticism against the Labour controlled Manchester City Council, and the more progressive elements of the now defunct Police Authority[8]. His views do not have the political coherence of those expressed by Conservative politicians or by some other leading police officers like London's Commissioner Newman. They are often exemplified by an absolute and primitive mistrust of politicians and an implacable sense of the moral authority which his force wields in his name over the pauperised communities of Manchester.

Anderton's personal crusade often finds itself running in tandem with the consensus of conservative opinion, but for the most part he is a man whose only real constituency is his police force. He is individual, emotional and messianic; an extremist in the most obvious sense of the word.

Anderton's deeply held subjective and sometimes contradictory views leave him isolated, and even mistrusted, by those who control the State with a colder and more scientific insight. He has frequently found himself at loggerheads with the majority of other chief officers in ACPO, although these struggles have never lessened his power within this organisation; he was described by another chief officer as holding a Svengali type sway over ACPO. During the miners' strike, he argued for the right to mobility for workers engaged in an industrial dispute when he voiced strong objections to the road blocks at the Dartford tunnel[9]. Faced with a long standing industrial dispute in Manchester, however, he mounted an SAS type operation to get new equipment through the pickets into the Lawrence Scott factory.

Many of the contradictions which Anderton articulates are in the realm of personal freedom and morality. When it comes to the guiding principles of State organisation and power, his views echo completely the lower middle class ideology of those who now represent the State. Because they are based upon gut reaction, and because his particular section of the class is not actually *in power,* he voices opinions that more careful Conservatives or industrialists only speak in private. He speaks of his dream of power with evangelical and almost biblical rhetoric:

> It will inevitably come to pass in all States clinging on to democracy that the survival of their ideals will increasingly depend upon the ability of *the police alone* to halt the risk of terrorism, serious crime and public disorder against which an uncompromising deterrent will be needed[10]. (author's italics)

Anderton's views are intensely political, often articulating the guiding philosophy of the post-industrial State in advance of its own theorists. In 1979, he said:

> I think that from a police point of view, *my* task in the future, in ten to fifteen years from now, *the period during which I shall continue to serve;* that basic crime as such—theft, burglary, even violent crime—will not be the predominant police feature. What will be the matter of greatest concern *to me* will be the covert and ultimately overt attempts to overthrow democracy, to subvert the authority of the State, and in fact, to involve themselves (sic) in acts of sedition designed to destroy our parliamentary system and the democratic government in this country[11]. (author's italics)

Anderton does not conceive of himself as a catcher of criminals in the older sense of the words. As a functionary of the new State, he has diagnosed the new crimes and he knows that as a post-industrial thieftaker, it will be his job to clean up those who criticise the State, or those whose social relations do not concur with those propagated by the State. Those who do not produce, and cannot be involved in exchange or consumption on any meaningful level, will have little social value and no social role; they will be subversive.

As they move closer to the centre of the State, police officers will no longer see their role as dealing with the rats-tails of disorder; the common criminal, the affray, or the break in. These menial jobs will be left to a lower class of officer. Elevated to the height of State power, the real and politicised police will be doing something else:

> The principal dilemma today is how best to reconcile essentially local policing, *requiring public co-operation*, understanding and support, with policing of a very different kind for which only professional police officers are adequately fitted.[12] (author's italics)

This new kind of police officer will inevitably operate outside the boundaries of our present democratic institutions or any other form of accountability; he will be political analyst, politician and police officer. The real policing will be carried out by a completely secret, highly politicised unpublic force, which will protect the State rather than the people; will defend the State against the people. Anderton is exceptionally clear about the sort of people who threaten the State and the nature of the democracy which is threatened:

> More and more people are less willing to comply with steps taken for the common good.[13]
>
> People must realise that when police have to resort to tougher tactics it is generally the fault of the community and not the struggling police.[14]

Just as the State detaches itself from the public whom it claims to represent; just as the police detach themselves from the community which they are meant to defend; so the State turns the responsibility of the individual citizen upon its head. People are not only the cause of their own condition; they also need protecting from themselves, appearing willing to give the State the stick with which to beat them.

> Policing will depend upon the mood of the people and *their willingness to be safely governed.*[15] (author's italics)

The modern police theorists of the right believe that the power of force is the only thing which will order the collapsing economic and social system. Having separated themselves from the people, the police can not now change sides. They have no choice but to support the State in attacking those who *do* defend themselves. The whole of the organised working and non-working population become the enemy:

> Mass picketing, if I can use that popular misnomer, and violent street demonstrations, *are acts of terrorism* without the bullet or the bomb. There must be few countries in the world prepared to watch, so patiently, a politically motivated industrial mafia (*sic: the working class represented as a criminal organisation*) at work, causing friction between the police and the people. I sometimes get a dreadful feeling that democracy, like the setting sun, is beginning to sink in the West. It is time we did something about it. [16] (author's italics).

The State itself is rarely defined in Anderton's analysis, but its enemies are often described to include those who live outside State institutions; marriage, the family, consumerism and heterosexual relationships. [17] Subversives become not only those who enter into a military or even political discourse with the institutions of power, but also those who criticise the State or live out unorthodox social relations, in particular social relations different from those manifest by the police:

> Extreme left wing groups, and factions in the ethnic minorities. *People who are permanently hostile to the police.*[18] (author's italics).

> I see in our midst an enemy more dangerous, insidious and ruthless than any faced since the second world war... a long term political strategy to destroy the proven structures *of the police.* (author's italics)

> In recent times there has been a most determined and sus-

> tained assault, hardly disguised, upon the independence and status of Chief Constables in particular, and the integrity of the service as a whole. *I believe it has been well organised as part of a wider plan to undermine the stability of the police service.* [19] (author's italics)

James Anderton's views are not just personal, they are the views of the Chief police officer of England's second largest constabulary and they are the most organised sum of all the other views held within his force. They are essentially ideological tenets, the less articulate themes of which can be traced through the culture and the politics of the whole force. When the Chief Constable enters the portals of the State, his army enters with him.

If the Chief Constable is to be an autonomous power, a person to whom, in Anderton's view, all civilian police workers should swear an oath of allegiance; if he is to be unaccountable to all democratic institutions; then those who serve under him deserve the same privilege. The Chief Constable comes to embody the values of the State and all his officers are awarded a similar authority. An attack upon the Chief Constable is an attack upon the State. An attack upon any officer in his force is a personal atack upon the Chief Constable *and* an attack upon the State.

In the Beginning: Confusion

At first nothing made sense in Manchester. Nothing seemed real. It was as if a community had been cast under a spell. So many people had peculiar stories to tell. Most odd were the stories that they didn't want to tell, or that finally, stutteringly, almost embarrassed, they began to tell. Then, they all began in the same way, as if you would think they were crazy.

"Look, I know that this sounds silly."

"We had a break in at our flat the other day and, well, I don't want to sound paranoid.

"Don't worry." You have to reassure them.

"Well, it was very odd, all the papers in my room were in a terrible state and an address book seems to be missing but...." Then he just blurted it out.

"But they only took a couple of sheets and a sauce pan."

It is important in such cases not to allow a silence to reach between the witness and yourself. You have to jump right in. As with all victims you have to explain, as best as you are able, that their condition is not an isolated one.

These people, students on the whole, came to us as if they had suffered a bereavement or had serious illnesses. Always they thought that their own reality was at fault, always they imagined that it had only happened to them.

For months we were in the dark about these things, like doctors at the beginning of an epidemic. A man whose flat overlooked the one lived in by Sarah Hollis and her friends, in the run down amphitheatre of John Nash Crescent, told us almost in a whisper about an incident:

"I was looking out of the window, it was one night a couple of weeks ago."

He fell silent and looked at his hands, then he took a deep breath and decided to say what was on his mind even if we thought he was crazy.

"There was always a car parked outside Sarah Hollis's flat, a mini, I imagined that it belonged to her. One day I saw a very new Ford in good condition drive slowly round the back of the flats and park behind the mini."

His confidence gave out on him and he paused again. He looked at us; it was obvious that he was trying to assess our belief in him; in people like him.

"Well, I know this sounds silly and I've thought about it over and over again. It was early evening, I know that I didn't dream it or imagine it."

He drew on his cigarette.

"Two well-dressed men, I'd swear they were police officers, got out of the Ford, went over to the mini and...."

It came out quickly, with all the words run together.

"And slashed the tyres."

Where is the reality within which we can place such reports. In the beginning it was like being given odd bits of an already completed jigsaw. The pieces you had been given were from the same jigsaw, but there was no place for them. We ended up taking out bits of the finished picture and changing the shape of the surrounding pieces so that ours would fit. Finally we finished the picture, all but a few pieces which we couldn't find; but the perspective and the significance of the new picture was radically different from the one which now lay in a heap next to it.

Looking back, although we were like doctors examining patients at the start of an epidemic, we had less chance of understanding the source of the outbreak or of containing it. The virus attacks without social or political reason and its course can be traced physically from one host to another. We of course knew the facts of crime, of burglary and vandalism, but we were slow in understanding how a criminal conspiracy was transmitted between police officers. We did not understand the motives of State employees, driven to secret conspiracies in order to obtain information and intelligence.

The young student stood there, her hands pushed firmly into the pockets of her jeans, her feet planted hard on the floor.

"Maybe I'm paranoid, but I don't think so."

She almost glared at us, with a look of challenging assertion; daring us to disbelieve her.

"In the early hours of this morning, someone smashed the quarterlight window of my car. Nothing was taken."

By the time she came to see us, we were learning fast and the new picture of the jigsaw was beginning to form a whole.

"Were you involved in the Leon Brittan demonstration, or have you been involved in either of the Inquiries?"

Now she looked perplexed.

"No."

"But...."

She went off into her own thoughts, her stance relaxed, now she was thinking things which she found unbelievable; her assertiveness had deserted her.

"A friend stayed at the flat last night, she has been very involved."

"Has this ever happened before,.... to your car?"

"No."

"Did you call the police?"

"Yes."

As if the penny had dropped, her face cleared of worry. Before we could talk her through it, she had reached her own conclusions.

"I had to so that I could claim the insurance. An officer came very quickly, I was surprised, with it being such a small matter. He stayed for quite a long time too and he asked questions about who lived in the house, who stayed in the house, whether we had any visitors. After a while he seemed less interested in the car window than in the occupants of the house."

The investigation spread and proliferated, until the investigators themselves were followed and harassed; this determination to control, this collation of intelligence, cannot be documented in a book of this kind. When it is printed on paper, the picture begins to fall apart again and the witnesses appear mad. This kind of conspiracy can only ultimately be felt by the people who suffer it.

Conspiracies are suffered as in a dream by their individual subjects; there is no collective understanding of a conspiracy because everyone draws the lines between the dots in a different fashion. The collective experience of conspiracy is shrouded in mist and each individual mind encounters black holes where they lack information.

The conspiracy in Manchester was big, and we, unlike the physicians have been unable to track it to its source or even find all the victims. Many who had only been touched by the infection thought that there was a greater sickness in believing and reporting the conspiracy than in suffering it.

Chapter one

Waiting for Leon

'Law and Order': these words have always had an ominous sound; the entire necessity and the entire horror of legitimate force are condensed and sanctioned in this phrase.

Herbert Marcuse: An Essay on Liberation

When the Conservative government came to office in 1979, at least one item of its manifesto was known to be problematic; education. Broadly speaking, the Conservatives wanted to massively cut the public bill for education while at the same time engineering a drift towards science subjects which would best service the needs of a post industrial, high technology economy. The vehicles for this policy were to be, on the one hand, the radical cutting of staff, buildings and student intake and on the other a gradual privatisation of both research funding and student grants. The latter, they hoped to accomplish through a voucher system, entailing loans from government or private industry which on completion of courses, would be paid back. Education was to be run for, and from, the private sector. The most plausible policies have obstacles, and less possible policies have even more.

Student intake was likely to be restricted, the tories thought, if fees were increased and grants reduced. Changes in course material could be effected by the curtailment of industrial and State grants to institutions for 'less necessary subjects,' as well as the gradual erosion of conditions of tenure and more stringent qualifications for academics who taught such courses. As the Conservatives moved from utopian capitalist theory to pluralist practice, the obstacles became evident. They confronted powerful lobbies from middle class parents whose class future was vested in the education of their children; from groups of progressive academics whose concerns were also not always philanthropic, and from an increasingly organised and vociferous student body who were willing to take to the streets.

Since the early seventies, students' unions, freed from the paternalism that had previously constrained them had grown not just into polical organisations but into business as well. Pushed hard to survive in the late seventies, many had taken on full time staff and branched out into investment and small business enterprises. Faced with well managed students' unions on a national and a local level, the government began to adopt methods which they had used before against industrially based trade unions. Central to their plans for breaking the students unions were the restriction of finances, and the use of the police to gain State ordered intervention in the universities.

It was the support which many student unions gave to the miners' strike, together with their campaigns against racism and other non-curricula issues which in the early eighties added a sense of urgency to Conservative thinking. Until the miners' strike government policies had met with a marked lack of success. During the strike, student activities gave the Tories a number of ideas to exploit. The first was ultra-vires payments; this was basically the same weapon that they used against the unions on the matter of the Labour Party levy and against the Local Authorities in the case of campaigns to democratise local government. Union activities could be restricted by a close and utilitarian monitoring of their funds.[20] On another front, and learning again from the miners' strike, the tories could set out to destroy the collectivity and organised power of the students by creating public order confrontations. Drawn into pickets and demonstrations students could be stigmatised not only because they appeared to be behaving in a way which was antithetical to the very concept of education, but they would also appear violent and undemocratic. Ultimately tory policies entailed sending in the 'State' in one form or another to control both the institutions of higher education themselves and the students unions in particular.

By December 1985, there had been, apparently, such an alarming number of violent incidents on university campuses, especially involving the picketing and barracking of government ministers, that the government was able to pressure the Vice Chancellors Committee into drawing up a set of guidelines restricting student protest and taking responsibility for disciplining students who protested against government policies.[21] It is unlikely that the government ever intended to allow these guidelines to be the principal authority over students. They reacted with patronising concern to what they considered to be the liberal inadequacy of the recommendations. By February 1986 stringent statutory means were being pushed on behalf of the government by its more lumpen back-benchers. A private members bill was proposed to 'safeguard the rights of free speech in Universities and Institutions of Higher Education.'[22]

The introduction of this Bill, moved by those members most demonstrated against by students, was dressed in the language beloved of the new conservatives since their campaigning days with the National Association For Freedom; 'any limiting of free speech should be done in the house and not by a *gang of fascists masquerading as students*.'[23]

The Bill fell at its second reading but thoroughout the first half of 1986 incident followed incident with increasing confusion and reported violence.[24] Finally the government felt obliged to incorporate clauses from the Bill into the Education Bill.[25] The clauses enforce the aquiescence of students and university administrations in unpopular and sometimes illegally expressed views which propound extreme right wing opinions. They place the onus upon the University administration to enforce discipline and to consult with the police in organising against those students who wish to demonstrate. These clauses in the Education Bill are a charter for right wing elements as well as simply unpopular conservative politicians to disturb the peace. They are an extension of the recently proposed public order legislation within the institutions of learning; in part they hand over the power of organised debate and dissent to the police, over the heads of Vice Chancellors and other administrators within higher education.

In March 1985, however, this process of politicising public order issues in the universities was still in its infancy. Michael Heseltine had been showered with red paint at Manchester in 1984, and in the early months of 1985, John Carlisle M.P. was kamikazeing his way round the country. On February 13th, he was punched and kicked at Bradford University as he touted his extremist views on building stronger links with South Africa. A week later, Leeds Polytechnic, worried about him disturbing the peace, posponed a planned visit. The Prime Minister took this opportunity to tell the Commons that 'freedom of speech is vital to our institutions of learning.' By March 1985 the scene was set for the visit of the Home Secretary to a University students' union which was already renowned for its uncompromising attitude to right wing speakers.

★ ★ ★

One day in September 1984, a member of the Conservative Student Association (CSA) at Manchester University opened the mail to find an official blue slip informing him that the Home Secretary would visit the students union in March 1985. His speech on 'Law and Order' would be the last engagement of a regional tour. Even the organiser for the CSA was surprised at the eminence of the visitor. Although they had submitted Brittan's name to the Conservative Party regional office as a requested speaker, no one had expected him to come.

It was unusual for M.P.'s with crowded agendas to speak at university students' unions; on the whole they preferred more politically productive venues. In September 1984, the miners' strike was at a crucial point and the Home Secretary was apparently immersed in overseeing its policing.

The students union's broad left executive officers and full time staff were informed of the visit early in 1985. They were not simply surprised but from the beginning concerned and worried, suspecting an ulterior motive in the visit. Nevertheless, the students' union began to make arrangements with a considered sense of responsibility. Not that there was any possibility of the union making independent decisions about anything relating to the visit; by January, an officer from Longsight police station had already asked for a meeting to discuss and organise security.

The first meeting between the police and executive members took place on February 15th, and this meeting was accepted as official confirmation of the visit. The manager of the union and the organiser for the CSA met with a police officer with the unlikely name of Ned Kelly. The meeting was informal and cordial. No minutes of this or other meetings were taken by the representatives of the students' union:

Following the meeting, the General Secretary and the union manager put certain plans to the union executive. Arrangements were made which covered security for the main debating hall; the use of union internal security staff; insurance and free access and exit from the hall. Security in the bars was discussed and the simple expediency, now common place, of replacing all glass ware and crockery by plastic, was agreed.

The students and officers who discussed these matters took cognizance of many factors which might affect the visit of a Home Secretary. Their security arrangements were exceptionally thorough. The union responsibility, it was decided, began inside the doors of the union building and from that point inwards, the union's own security staff would oversee the visit and the meeting. At later meetings with the police it was agreed that specialised police would be present at the door of the meeting to search the audience. Special Branch personnel protecting the Home Secretary would be allowed into the meeting.

The distribution of tickets for the occassion was to be strictly controlled. Fifty tickets would be given to the CSA. Others were to be given out through the union shop, on the basis of one ticket per person. To ensure that no one received more than one ticket each recipient would have his or her union card hole-punched as evidence of receipt.

The next meeting between the students and the police took place on February 21st, in the early afternoon. Inspector Kelly and Superintendent John Hall attended from Longsight police station. Again, this was an informal and cordial meeting. The union's plans were presented to the police for approval. The police appeared quite happy; and in the general discussion, two other points of agreement were reached. None of the students or their officers could have known that one of these decisions was crucial to the way in which the visit of the Home Secretary was to be policed. The police asked casually that the steps of the union building be regarded just for the night, as a public highway. The students agreed. In terms of public order law and police authority, they had just ceded their right to lawfully demonstrate on their own private property. The police for their part, having just gained control by 'gentleman's' agreement of the private property of the union, promised that they would deploy a minimal presence of ten officers 'immediately outside the front doors' of the building. Quite sure that this was a fair agreement, the students also asked the police to keep any presence of uniformed officers inside the union building to a minimum.

On February 26th., the head of the university security staff, with other university officers, met with the Manager of the union. At this meeting, the union requested the removal of paving stones, and any other material which could be used as missiles, from the immediate area of the union building.

In the next four days, a number of other meetings took place between the General Secretary of the union and the police. At one, eight police officers were present, a number of them specialists who did not disclose their area of concern. At another, a tour of potential 'trouble spots' was undertaken.

Two or three days prior to the visit of the Home Secretary, a decision was made by the union executive to lock the doors to the union building immediately prior to the visit. The General Manager of the union informed the police of this decision.

Now, looking back on the arrangements for the visit, no one seems to remember who it was that was so insistent that Leon Brittan enter through the front doors of the union. The organiser for the CSA remembers having discussed this matter with the Conservative regional office. He thinks that it was generally agreed that despite the decision of the students to hold a picket on the steps, such an eminent person should not be asked to enter through any other door. Only a few weeks previously, Leon Brittan had visited London University's Queen Mary College; there, in the face of a relatively small gathering of students, he and his retinue had had no difficulty in deciding to enter the building unobserved through a side entrance.

In the early afternoon of March 1st, on the istructions of the union executive, the Manager rang Longsight Police Station to inform the police that the executive had released a press statement requesting the Home Secretary to enter through another door. The police rang back to say that there was no possibility of complying with this request. About three quarters of an hour before the Home Secretary was due to arrive, police officers began to enter the union building. They did not keep their presence to a minimum and they were far from unobtrusive. Parts of the building were taken over by them with officers positioning themselves strategically on the stairs and in the corridors.

At the front of the building also, officers were not keeping to the part of the agreement which seemed advantageous to them, that the steps be considered a part of the public highway and that ten officers position themselves immediately in front of the doors. Instead of controlling the steps from the beginning and marshalling the demonstration from the top, officers were standing by in a relaxed manner and allowing a crowd of three hundred students to block the 'highway'. Senior police officers watched as an impenetrable body of demonstrators built up between the doors of the union and the pavement where the Home Secretary would step from his car.

Many students who had not been present at any negotiations with the police imagined that the Home secretary had after all decided to enter the building by another less public route.

All the Necessary Steps

In March 1985, Steven Shaw was a third year student at Manchester University, taking a degree in politics and philosophy. The next four months would be the most difficult of his university course; not only did he have his final examinations in June but he had to finish a 15,000 word thesis by the end of the term. He had chosen to do his thesis on police technology and surveillance.

Steve was twenty two; one of two sons and a daughter of a working class Jewish family in London. His father Maurice, a taxi driver, was one of eight children born in the poorest part of London's East End. His mother, Helen a woman quickly coming to terms with a modern role, was also from a traditional Jewish area of East London, where her father had been a furniture maker. Steve's was a caring family, and though not involved in politics they, like many such families with origins in East London, believed in playing their part in the community.

Before university, Steve had been interested in swimming and had swum for a national youth team. A lose limbed, bulky lad, he didn't walk or look like an athlete, despite his broad shoulders and good build. Nearly six foot tall, he moved almost awkwardly with a large loose clumsiness. To those who knew him, he appeared unassertive and perhaps soft, always eager to find out others' opinions. He presented a picture, like his father, of a caring and emotional person; giving off an air of warmth and easy affability.

Since the beginning of his time at university Steve had taken a peripheral interest in politics; he wasn't committed to any group or faction, but like many of the other students that he mixed with, he took a keen interest in the society around him. His interest in politics is perhaps best described by a student friend of his; 'He was essentially an academic, he knew a great deal about different political systems, but he was not as actively involved as some other students. He was particularly interested in Latin American politics and the effects of imperialism. He worked in anti-racist campaigns and had naturally developed an interest in the quickly changing role of the police. In fact, he was little different from thousands of other young people who find themselves emotionally and intellectually drawn towards the left.

Over the previous weeks, Leon Brittan's visit had been widely advertised within the university and there was no shortage of people wanting to demonstrate against his presence. Brittan had overseen a continuous and almost military police campaign against the miners during their year long strike. The students who had decided to assemble on the steps of the union building hoped to make a public and *legal* show of their opposition to Brittan and the Conservative government. Although the visit had been widely publicised, little or no organisation had gone into the demonstration.

Steve arrived at the union building about six o'clock. There were only thirty or so students around and he knew most of them. It was a dull damp evening. He hadn't been to many demonstrations and he wondered how many people would turn up before Brittan came. He wasn't particularly interested in the police; he certainly didn't see the demonstration as part of his work.

During the day he had noticed plain clothes officers inside the union building, watching people, and he presumed that they had stayed inside. Outside on the steps, a small number of uniformed officers milled around exchanging comments with the demonstrators.

Over the next hour the crowd got bigger and banners and placards went up, a student arrived with a loud hailer and the picket began to get more animated. Steve wandered around the edge of the steps speaking to friends. At this point, he noticed what he assumed to be plain clothes officers working their way into the crowd, speaking to each other, looking casual, their hands in jacket pockets. He didn't give them too much thought because they just might have been students that he had not seen before.

Suddenly, at ten minutes past seven, a large group of police officers pushed into the demonstration and began clearing the steps.

All at once there was the crushing weight of three hundred young people, jostling and turning, trying to keep their feet. He couldn't see what was happening at the point where the police confronted the students, and as the crowd was pushed back up the steps, he went with them. As the centre of the steps cleared, he found himself near the top facing a police cordon. There was a great deal of noise and the weight of people behind him pushed him against the police lines.

He didn't have the energy or the space to shout and tried to concentrate on keeping his feet and not getting crushed. Officers at the front of the lines were grabbing students all around him, dragging them from the crowd and pushing them down the steps. Suddenly, a police officer grabbed his leg and he was thrown off balance, backwards and down. People in the crowd behind him held his arm and shoulders while the police officer now joined by others pulled him three or four feet down the steps. Everything was confusion, he was conscious of swearing and shouting but all he could see were people's legs and feet and the dark sky overhead.

The conflagration finished as suddenly as it had begun. One of his shoes split and came away from his foot; the officers pulling at him fell back into clear space. Steve was retrieved by the crowd and brought to his feet. Within five minutes the police had established cordons from the top of the steps down both sides and the students, though still shouting, now particularly at the police, shook themselves down and tried to create space for themselves. Steve peered tentatively over the cordon in search of his shoe. When he saw it he shouted good humouredly, though rather embarassed, to an officer who picked it up and passed it over to him.

He felt sore and shaken from his fall on the steps. From where he stood, he saw an Asian man dragged away by the hair and he saw others, students, firmly grasped and marched away under arrest. He stood and shouted as Leon Brittan was escorted into the union building and then decided to leave.

Steve met up with a woman friend and they walked away from the steps on to the opposite side of Oxford Road and down Dover Street. Half way down Dover Street, they passed the police assembly point. There were five or six blue militarised Tactical Aid Group vans, police dogs and a number of uniformed officers. The officers were having a bit of a laugh, playing around and shouting at each other.

Steve and his friend caught a bus and went off into a normal Manchester night, to a house in Longsight.

Back in the small terraced house which his friend rented with other women they all talked about the picket. Others had seen more than Steve and had been disturbed by the violence of the police. Later that evening they watched the television news, which showed clearly what had happened; how the police had waded into the students, thrown, pushed and battered them down the steps. Not surprisingly, the commentary did not really co-incide with the pictures. From the description alone it would have been easy to get the impression that hundreds of students, trying to attack the Home Secretary, had fought a pitched battle with the police.

Neither Steven or any of the others watching the television were aware of the smaller and still unrecorded details of that night's demonstration. They did not know for example that one television crew had switched off their cameras the moment that the police charged the steps.

But even without knowing these details, some began to understand more clearly what might have happened on miners' picket lines throughout the last year.

Chapter Two

The Monstrous Regiment

If we fail to keep the rules and thereby achieve victory by surprise, that is a demonstration of our military skill; if they fail to keep the rules and thereby achieve victory by surprise that is a demonstration of their military barbarity

Edmund Leach: Custom, Law and Terrorist Violence

Manchester has one of the biggest higher education complexes in europe. Within half a mile there are two universities and a polytechnic, with a total of over 30,000 students. At most periods during term time students can be seen walking in droves along the main road which passes their buildings, to lecture rooms, libraries and labs. Loaded with books and bags they stand on the pavement in small groups making arrangements and arguing course content. In the mornings they stream from the surrounding bed-sitter areas like their factory counterparts in industrial cities did fifty years ago.

Students in any large city are similar, with an easily discernable culture and a commitment which has little in common with the propaganda put out about them by an older and usually male political establishment. They learn under pressure, conscious not only of their responsibility to their families and to the next generation, but equally aware of the gathering economic crisis. Like all sections of the population they have felt this crisis in real terms. And although 'student politics' might traditionally have been viewed with some cynicism, their struggles in recent years over their own financial and educational conditions have matured their politics and political structures. Increasing State intervention, cutbacks, and constant attacks on the tenure and status of teaching personnel, have often thrown together lecturers and students in common cause against the present Conservative government.

The Manchester University students union building sits squat and white on the edge of the city centre. Together with other university buildings, it marks the southern end of the old civic centre and the beginning of the inner city. Further south along Oxford Road is Rusholme, a jumbled area of new Asian shops, restaurants and student accommodation.

The union building is bland and solid. The wide, shallow, stone steps leading up to its doors are divided by two ramparts and contained by two more at either end. The large metal framed windows above the first floor overlook Oxford Road from a bar and various leisure rooms.

March 1st. 1985 was a typical Manchester Friday; damp and dismal. Plain clothes police officers walked about freely within the union building. Unfamiliar amongst the young people, they watched as students met and organised; they spied upon students in communal areas. For some of the politically active students, it was already a day of tension, the court had just begun sitting again after an adjournment in the Jackie Berkeley trial. A small number of students were backwards and forwards between Manchester Magistrates Court, and the union building. Some of them had taken the case very seriously; one young woman had attended court every day to write a full transcript. A number of the students who were to attend the demonstration that evening had been regular visitors to the court; they had all been watched and observed by the police over a period of weeks.

The Berkeley case was not the only catalyst that had awakened an awareness in students to the activities of the Manchester police. During the grants campaign of 1984, a number of students had been arrested on a demonstration which ended up outside Manchester town hall. Some of those arrested had been violently abused; one young woman had two front teeth knocked out. These events, together with the students economic conditions and their close geographical proximity to the black and Asian communities, mixed with a critique of sexual politics, had developed a critical consciousness about police attitudes and behaviour.

On the evening of March 1st, students began to assemble on the steps outside the student union building at about six o'clock. By 6.30 pm., a handful of police officers, who attracted little attention, stood on the pavement talking amongst themselves and consulting with Special Branch officers who came and went about their 'important' business. Other officers reconnoitered the back and sides of the building.

Plain clothes officers with two way radios had by this time stationed themselves in various rooms at the front of the building, from where they had a clear view of the steps. There was no tension or anger as the demonstration began to assemble. Students mixed easily with the police who stood on the pavement at the bottom of the steps and oversaw the crowd which was also assembling on the opposite side of the road.

As seven o'clock approached, a television crew arrived; this sparked off a more vociferous reaction than had the small number of police. A student with a megaphone led the chanting against the media, and at the bottom of the steps, one sergeant, part of a small command group of three officers, made up his mind to arrest him before the night was out.

What was soon to happen to the students gathered on the steps of their union building was outside their previous experience, none of them could have foreseen that this small demonstration would be used as an experimental model for para-military policing. Nor could they have known that these steps, so comfortably full of joking and chanting students, would shortly be turned into a whirlpool of violence. Had the students thought more about the situation, and the identity of the expected visitor, they might have surmised that some ceremony, a symbolic show of efficiency, was likely to be in the minds of senior Manchester police officers. Some might also have wondered why, with three hundred of them now packing the steps and one hundred and fifty on the opposite pavement, there was only a handful of police officers present.

Few students were taking much notice of police preparations. Later on an inquiry would be faced with the problem of having to validate insubstantial and diffused memories. Ominous signs of police preparation did not, however, go completely unnoticed:

> Before the police went into the crowd on the steps, I saw plain clothes police walking up and down outside the union with long truncheons like baseball bats.[26]

The students, now packed tightly on the steps, were pushed up against the closed union doors at the top, standing on the concrete ramparts and milling around the edges of the steps onto the pavement and the grass at their sides. There was a confusing array of placards and slogans, but the chanting signalled a developing sense of collectivity.

The first arrest of the evening took place not in the vicinity of the steps but round the back of the union building. Negotiations between the students' union and the police had left some with the impression that the Home Secretary would enter by the back entrance. One student had been posted at the back of the building with a two way radio, to inform the demonstration if Brittan entered that way.

This student was arrested by uniformed officers around 6.45 p.m.; another, who went to the scene of the arrest, was told by an Inspector and a sergeant that he had been arrested on suspicion of theft. Despite receipts being produced for the two way radio, the arrested student was kept in custody until about 9.00 p.m., when he was finally released without charge.

By 7.10 p.m., the demonstration on the steps was as large as it would get. The picket was well under way and the placards showed an array of motives for attendance; some students protested against the government's immigration policies; others wanted to make their voice heard about the policing of the miners' strike; a group of women students were campaigning against the tax on tampons. The whole demonstration was united under a single banner which hung from the first floor railings of the union building: SUPPORT THE MINERS ONE YEAR ON.

Around seven o'clock one demonstrator arrived with a report of police organisation down a side street across Oxford Road:

> I was walking down Dover Street towards Oxford Road just before 7.15 pm. I saw several police vans and about forty officers lined up in two's in Portsmouth Street.

By this time, the students were in complete occupation of the steps, although their occupation was not to them a strategic imperative. They were not organised to defend the steps; they simply wanted to express their distaste for the Home Secretary and the policies of his government. The union building and the steps which led up to it were by rights if not by police agreement, their property and they were obstructing neither the footpath nor the highway. The few police officers nearby were still reasonable and discursive. But while the students were in a state of blissful ignorance about what had been planned for them, the police officers were fully aware of the strategy which was about to be carried out by their fellow officers. No doubt there were those amongst them who were comforted by the knowledge that a large squad of Tactical Aid officers was soon to come in and 'do the business.'

Unnoticed by the majority of the students, a number of plain clothes officers had by this time established themselves within the demonstration. These men and women, dressed in casual clothes similar to those worn by the students, were operating in pairs.

By ten past seven, the evening had turned dark and drizzly. The occupants of the steps shuffled about trying to keep warm. There was a clamour of noise as they talked and shouted. Then those at the northern end of the steps and in the front rows of the crowd at the bottom began to discern two columns of police marching in military style along the wet road. These officers looked ahead expressionlessly as the sound of their boots became louder. Students who saw them approaching assumed that they would form a cordon at the base of the steps or perhaps assemble in front and await instructions. None of the students showed any signs of fear or panic.

> At 7.10 pm., I noticed about 40 police come scrambling out of the vans in Lime Grove and Dover Street, meet in the centre of Oxford Road, stop the traffic, then form into a column two abreast walking down the centre of Oxford Road.

When the column reached the steps, it turned, the officers marching at a 'purposeful walk or a slow trot, not running.' The officer at their head threaded his way through two or three rows of students, dividing them with his hands. Then the assault began. Officers at the head of the serial[27], behind the commanding Inspector, began to force their way up the steps. Fists and feet flying, they pressed into the unsuspecting and undefended gathering of young men and women.

No warnings were issued, no instructions given; the officers simply attacked those in front of them and fought their way up the steps. They punched students indiscriminately, kicked them, and threw them bodily down the steps. Some of those thrown to the ground were then pounced on by other officers who began to drag, pummel and kick them. Both male and female students were grabbed around the

SUPPORT THE MINERS ONE YEAR ON

neck, dragged by the hair or simply thrown from one officer to another until they landed on the road immediately in the path of oncoming traffic.

The students were utterly unprepared for the onslaught or its ferocity; they had neither the organisation, the audacity nor the weaponry to fight back. Nowhere in the crowd was there any physical resistance. One student did manage to throw a pint of orange juice over an officer and a few others bravely tried to land punches on their assailants:

> Initially there was some pushing from the crowd of students, but this soon ceased as it became obvious the degree of violence that the police were prepared to use, and besides, some people had fallen to the ground and the body of demonstrators seemed to show some concern for human life, even if the police did not.
>
> ★
>
> The initial student response was to push forwards. However, this push was short lived as a number had collapsed under the pressure. The students began to to be compressed on the steps as the police drove forwards.
>
> ★
>
> They did not give any warning. They just ploughed through the picket up the steps, pushing, shoving, throwing people out of their way. When one of them got to where I was, he said, "Move before you get your fucking head kicked in." I saw one girl thrown backwards down the right side of the steps. One of the police pulled me by the lapels out of the crowd and said, "I don't want to see you here again. If you want to be a fucking martyr I'll arrest you." Later, I saw a picket being repeatedly elbowed in the face, the officer concerned said words to the effect, "Sorry, I didn't see you there."
>
> ★
>
> I saw one man being pummelled by a police officer as he

staggered down the steps. The man tumbled down, his arm raised against his face as some kind of protection. The policeman fell on him and continued punching.

★

A black man had his glasses ripped off and hurled to the ground by a policeman.

★

I witnessed two girls being dragged out by their hair and reduced to tears. I saw several people kicked and punched down the stone steps. Several plain clothes police were indulging in gross physical violence. In the crush when Brittan arrived I witnessed one officer removing a girl from the crowd, calling her "nigger," and saw him hit her while dragging her towards the van.

★

I saw one policeman who seemed to be moving away from the crowd turn suddenly and attack a male student directly in front of us. He punched the student in the head and then proceeded to drag him forcibly down the steps by his hair, aided by about four other officers.

★

A policeman grabbed hold of the back of my head and pulled me down; I was then punched in one eye and several times in the stomach. After this, I was picked up and thrown down the steps.

★

I saw one police officer drag a member of the crowd from the Union side of Oxford Road to my side and push him into the crowd of spectators. I saw a second officer who had seen the first officer push the man into the crowd, then go up to the man, who was walking away, and thump him fairly violently.

★

I was violently removed by a policeman grabbing my throat and pushing me down the steps. I rollled down to be grabbed by the throat again and punched back into the road.

★

I was punched in the face by an officer, which sent me falling down the steps, a witness to this was also punched in the face and his glasses smashed. Later an officer punched another male student in the mouth and I was punched in the eye.

The push up the steps, was, for the police, a clear victory. Once the majority of officers had reached the top of the steps, other officers flowed in behind them in two ranks, pushing the divided halves of the demonstration to the top and sides of the steps. Students Union executive members and the building's internal security officers locked all three doors at the the top of the steps to stop students from coming into the building. On one side of the steps, the pressure on the rampart was such that the hand rail which is riveted to the wall collapsed and a number of students fell about four feet onto the bikes parked below.

There was nowhere for the students to go, they could not turn behind themselves into the union building because the doors were locked and even if they had been able to, the fighting which would have ensued as the police tried to occupy the building would have made what happened on the steps look like a nursery. They could not move to the sides because of the crush against the ramparts and the railings. They fell hopelessly, like nine pins, at the hands of the police, who flung bodies the only way they could go, behind them and down the stone steps.

Then the police moved up the steps and I saw one policeman use his helmet as a flail and strike out with it. He was on the right side of the formation. He took hold of the helmet by the strap, I saw it being used, it was striking upwards above his head.

It was a debacle. Once the centre of the steps had been cleared of bodies, the police picked off stragglers and those who had managed to escape the initial onslaught. With the students hemmed in by cordons on the right and the left of the steps, officers threw punches with gloved fists over the lines at any face which was near enough for them to reach.

> A policeman with no provocation kicked the girl standing next to me in the shins. He quickly stepped back into the cordon and stood smiling. He refused to give his number.
>
> ★
>
> The policemen were in formation and pushing us in the chest. One knocked a cigarette out of my mouth then hit me in the face.

As things began to settle, as students sought medical help or were arrested and thrown into vans, the scene on the steps resembled a deserted battle field.

> After the assault, there were shoes, a scarf, glasses and an ear-ring lying on the ground that had been cleared. A police officer picked up a watch (chromium bracelet, analog and digital) and said to his friend, "This must be one of our lot's" and put it in his pocket[28].

There were in fact few arrests during the drive up the steps. The operation was not a 'legal' one against people committing a criminal act. The main purpose of the police assault was to clear the steps by force. Those who were thrown to the bottom of the steps found themselves manhandled and perhaps arrested; a few who escaped the assault and found themselves in free space were also arrested.

In March 1985 Sarah Hollis was a twenty three year old second year medical student. Her father's vocation as a minister with a Suffolk parish in the south of England, and her mothers example of Christian values, had instilled in her a sense of service to the community. She was a member of the Student Union Council and Christians in Politics. A short, stocky and robust young woman, she had a strong

sense of her own individuality and a busily efficient attitude towards life. Like Steven Shaw she was interested in sport, playing hockey in a mixed university team; she was not, on the surface at least, intimidated by the physical strength of men.

On March 1st, she had arrived at the union building at five o'clock with her ticket to ensure that she got a place in the debating hall. On her arrival, however, she was approached by a member of the union executive who asked for her help in handing out uncollected tickets to members of the CSA. For a quarter of an hour before seven o'clock she stood in the foyer of the union handing out tickets. Through the windows in the doors to the building she could see the demonstration assembling.

Just after seven o'clock it was evident to those inside the foyer that there was trouble on the steps outside. Standing on a chair, Sarah could see over the heads of the crowd on the steps. She saw the police fighting their way up to the top; she saw officers hitting out at people, students screaming in panic and others being crushed against the doors.

Inside the building, when other members of the students union could see what was happening, an emergency executive meeting was held in one of the corridors leading off the foyer. The discussion centred upon whether it was still possible, in light of the police behaviour, to ring Longsight Police Station and cancel the meeting. They finally decided that it should go ahead.

The Home Secretary's car parked against the pavement at the base of the steps at about 7.30pm. Brittan was dragged out of his car to camera flashes and the weird glow of television lights. Officers from the Tactical Aid Group assembled in a 'V' formation on the pavement, the foremost and fattest officer hitching up his pants before the scrummage. Brittan was thrown like a lump of lard sticking in a waste pipe, into the neck of the 'V'. Large numbers of Special Branch officers jammed themselves between the two wings of the 'V' and the whole monstrous regiment heaved and trundled, panting, to the top of the steps. Much pomp and little ceremony made the scene reminiscent of a male party game.

On both sides of the steps, at a distance, students, provoked and angered at the violence used by the police, shouted a barrage of obscenities and abuse at Brittan. At the top of the steps the Home

Secretary was precipitated through the doors of the union building where he and his entourage tried to regain whatever composure they might previously have possessed.

Inside the debating hall, Brittan met fierce but only verbal resistance to his attempts to speak. Women at the back of the room turned their backs on him and sang while others maintained a barrage of noise. Only a fraction of the speech remains for posterity, partly recorded by one of the students who had managed to get in after first standing on the steps outside.

> I actually went inside and addressed the meeting. I asked Leon Brittan specifically if he knew what was going on outside, but the microphone which I had been given was cut off and he interrupted, calling all those outside 'red fascist scum'[29].

Outside the building, the police embarked upon a second wave of arrests as they pushed students further down the steps and cordoned them round the corners of the steps onto the pavement.

> After the Home Secretary entered the union building the police started to arrest people for the most dubious reasons; saying things to friends; complaining about the lack of freedom of speech. Others were chased, punched and kicked by groups of four or five officers.
>
> ★
>
> I was walking away from the union because I was going to meet my girl friend later that evening. However, as I came abreast of the police vans which were lined up along Oxford Road, I saw three or four police officers tackling a man and pushing him to the ground with what I believed to be unnecessary force, I lost my cool for a moment and shouted out, "That's dead hard isn't it? That's dead hard". At that point, I was grabbed from behind by a plainclothes man, marched a few feet to the police van and shoved in.

Brittan's exit from the building was thoroughly planned. Just before he left the debating room, officers from the steps marched into the building and took control of all the strategic points inside. A number of officers occupied the first floor bar, standing in front of the windows overlooking the steps; the corridors were cleared and points of entry into the foyer were blocked off by police. Brittan had a clear but hurried run down the stairs, through the foyer and out down the steps.

> Later while Leon Brittan was speaking, I went into the first floor bar. I stood by one of the windows along the front of the room. Police came in and stood, two to each window, and encouraged the people watching to move away.
>
> ★
>
> I went up to the Serpent Bar, bought a drink and sat down. As Brittan's speech was ending, about thirty policemen entered the bar and lined up in front of the windows. The police remained in the bar for approximately five minutes after Brittan had gone. Eventually, after some verbal abuse from the students, they left.

When Brittan left at 8.25 pm, hurried out in the same undignified way that he had arrived, many of the students expected the police to disappear into the darkness, leaving them to piece together their lives in the safety of their own building. But it was after Brittan had gone that the most violent events of the evening occurred. By this time, the police evidently considered that it was part of their duty to rid the whole area of students.

> A friend of mine was arrested for shouting at Brittan as he left.
>
> ★
>
> Although Leon Brittan had left, the police stayed for about half an hour and a dozen more arrests were made.

The steps and the union building had now become what the police refer to as a 'symbolic location'. The potency of that symbol, the ownership of the steps, and the memory of the assault, had to be fractured and diffused. The police did not want students hanging about, talking, planning and perhaps demonstrating or marching against them. The area had to be cleared, returned to its neutral stone, and the remaining students pushed back into the isolation of their individual accommodation.

The final denouement was still to come. With the steps cleared of everything but litter and with a few officers standing at the top, others pushed, punched and shepherded students along the pavement of Oxford Road. With Brittan no doubt happily speeding towards Manchester Airport, a group of police officers and students made their way out of the foyer and on to the top of the steps. Charles Alcock, an executive officer of the union began to remonstrate with the few remaining officers about what had happened.

> I shouted towards the officers, "It's all over, just go, leave the building now, it's all over, leave our building, don't ever come back." Immediately, a policeman grabbed me round the neck and began to drag me down the steps. I was grabbed by some friends. The two sides tugged me and I fell to the ground. My friends implored the officers that I had done nothing. By then, three officers had grabbed me by the hair. As they tugged me down the steps they banged my head against them. Then I was tugged to my feet, held leaning forward and punched twice in the face until my face bled from the nose.

It was by now dark and fairly desolate around the steps, the night was at a tired end as the police at the top of the steps moved in again. It was then that Sarah Hollis became an accidental witness to the assault on Charles Alcock with whom she was leaving the building.

> I proceeded down the stairs from the MDH (Main Debating Hall) and into the foyer. At this point, there were about a dozen police officers walking ahead of us and out of the building. The police seemed relaxed and were walking out in a casual manner. On reaching the top of the union steps

> I and other students about me stopped. I heard a male friend of mine shout something to the effect that the police had done their job and that they should get out of our union as they were not wanted there. Immediately, a policeman turned round and grabbed him round the neck; straight away, other policemen converged on him and others who were standing near him, including me. I was extremely distressed because policemen were hitting my friend, pulling his hair and wrenching his head. I screamed out not to hurt him and reached out to grab him. At this point, a policeman grabbed me by the hair. I felt my head being jerked back which caused me great pain in my neck and then felt myself projected down the steps, striking my head on one of the steps as I fell. I then lost consciousness.

It would only become apparent later that anyone who had knowledge of this incident, and in fact anyone who had any specific knowledge of the events of that night, was in danger. One witness to the attack upon Sarah Hollis made a statement to the defence campaign on March 3rd. Her name was Jeanette, her address was at the top of the statement.

> On the demonstration on the union steps on Friday 1st March 1985, I saw a police officer grab hold of Sarah Hollis from behind and throw her down the steps away from the doors. She was knocked unconscious. I was pushed away from the scene by two officers so that I tripped and fell. Police surrounded Sarah in order to push the crowd back. Not one of them went to her aid at this point.

This final conflict at the top of the steps involved officers already on the steps and a small group who were on their way out of the foyer. It was very violent and completely provoked by the police.

> There were officers in front of me and officers behind me and we walked out through the main centre doors. Charlie was saying "Would you go now, please just go out of the building," not aggressively or provocatively, "Leave us

alone to sort out what has happened.'' He was then grabbed by a group of police officers, 3,4, or 5. There was a lot of commotion on the steps. I saw him being grabbed forward and they tried to pull him down the steps. I saw him being grabbed by his hair. There was a sudden surge of pressure from behind and I lost balance and lost sight of Sarah. The police pulled me up by my hair at the bottom of the steps, the police officer shoved my arms up behind my back. At this stage I saw Sarah just lying on the pavement.

★

Maybe five minutes after, the police started walking out of the building. There was no pushing or shoving. I then went out to the top of the steps of the union building and was joined by Charles Alcock. A single police officer walked past and got to the top of the steps, at which stage Charlie shouted. This particular policeman just stopped, turned round, looked at Charlie, got hold of him by the back of the hair, twisted him round, got him in an arm lock and proceeded to drag him down the steps. The officer then came rushing back. I couldn't follow the incident from then on, as behind me there was another student and as I looked round, there was a policeman with his fist raised ready to strike the student; I put my hand up and told him to stop, at which stage the policeman withdrew and then I saw the whole crowd of people tumble down the steps.

★

I got one student back inside and then I saw an officer hitting him with the brim of of a helmet. He was holding the student's head and the back of the helmet was being used on the students head. He was holding it by the brim and chopping across the top of the head.

Senior officers and members of the Tactical Aid Group worked hard to stop any of Sarah's friends from reaching her as she lay unconscious on the pavement. In battles of this kind involving the police, symbols as well as material objects and space have to be either

OLICE

destroyed or recuperated; this is how the propaganda battle is won.

Something had gone badly wrong. While the police knew from training and long experience that they would be able to explain away blows to arrested students by claiming that students had assaulted them; while it might be possible to justify the initial charge on the basis of the danger the demonstration presented to the Home Secretary; how was it going to be possible to explain away the serious injury of a young student who now lay dramatically unconscious at the bottom of the steps. One act of violence too many might have precipitated another Blair Peach scandal; another death at the hands of the police.

While Senior officers knelt in attendance on Sarah, they must have been praying that she wasn't seriously injured, that she wouldn't die on them. The whole future and deployment of the Tactical Aid group depended upon its officers carrying out an efficient operation while hiding their violence. The serious injury of a young woman could not be considered an efficient resolution to the evenings deployment. But the individual constable responsible probably had more personal worries on his mind. He would not however have to worry unduly, his comrades would surely muster alibis for him; after all, they were all in it together doing their job. It could have happen to any of them.

By the following morning, it was clear that a 'damage limitation' operation was underway, the Daily Mail carried a picture of Sarah Hollis' unconscious body surrounded by police officers with the caption: 'Police aid demo girl.'

Chapter Three

Defending the Person of the State

If you're black or unemployed
Then you won't be overjoyed
To feel my boot in contact
With your knee (at least).
With my fists I've tried to prove
My talent for a move
To the company police, the SPG.

Mike Carver: The SPG Song (a thug's lament)

The police were aware of the visit of Leon Brittan to the students' union at least two months before it occurred. In the months before the visit, senior officers from 'A' Division headquarters, Bootle Street police station and from Longsight held meetings with both the General Manager and the General Secretary of the Students Union, together with the organiser of the CSA. The parties however, were not really communicating with each other. The union knew full well that any agreement reached with the police was likely to be broken. The police knew that whatever the assurances given by the officers and the executive members of the union they did not want to police their students members.

While the student body organised to picket the union building, the police organised to effect a safe and undisturbed entry for the Home Secretary. This they did with a total disregard for the student's rights. By acting in a military fashion, they managed to turn a peaceful picket into a trial of strength between the power of the State and the right of democratic dissent. The police saw the situation from the beginning, not so much as one of 'public order'—for this, after all, could have been simply resolved by Brittan attending another building or by a negotiated settlement with the union executive, allowing both the right to demonstrate and the right to speak—but one of military logistics. In effect the police chose to seize and occupy the union building and its immediate environs.

Certain officers within every constabulary force are trained and continually active in the kind of military operation which was planned that night. These officers and their units have a variety of names in different constabularies; a diversity which is more by design than by accident. Brought together as they were during the miners' strike, they comprise a 'third force', or a national riot police[30]. In the Greater Manchester Police area this para-military force is called the Tactical Aid Group (TAG).

TAG is one of a number of such units set up since 1965. Following the adverse publicity which surrounded them throughout the seventies, their military titles have dropped out of use and there is now a bias amongst the police establishment towards calling them all by the neutral term Police Support Units (PSU).

TAG is a force wide organisation; a force within a force. It can be called into any division on the basis of need. It is answerable only to a small number of senior officers and a communications headquarters. Officers from the group are not always deployed in public order situations nor are they always in uniform. Teams of TAG officers might be used in sieges, to escort marches and oversee demonstrations, or to flood areas of high crime and mount undercover surveillance for car thefts and burglaries.

Officers undergo extensive team training in para-military manoeuvres, the use of firearms, baton rounds and gas; their instructors are sometimes from the army and much of their terminology and tactics are based upon armed forces 'internal security' operations. Although units train together and there is a special emphasis placed upon co-ordinated military strategies, after their term of duty TAG officers drop back into normal policing duties and will then form part of the trained back up of PSU's available in times of crisis[31].

The impression is often given that there are only a limited number of para-military trained officers available in special squads, within each constabulary, at any given time. The object of training and rota deployment is, however, to train all officers between certain ages in para-military tactics. Over the last ten years, massive resources have been poured into building this dual policing function within each constabulary. The police have essentially been trained as a standing army to obviate the need to bring the army on to the streets.

In Greater Manchester, TAG units are conveyed in dark blue militarised carriers wth slide back iron meshing over the windscreens and smoke black windows. They train, plan and travel in units of eleven constables with one sergeant to every two units. The carriers are Sherpas, especially converted at some expense (£10,480) to carry weapons and riot policing equipment. Manchester has a fleet of six carriers which they are enlarging to sixteen. These carriers, with their units, are currently based at Haywood, Stretford and Longsight police stations, two units working from each station. When other PSU's aid TAG officers on any specific operation, they travel in either white Sherpa vans or police buses.

The operational control room for TAG is at Stretford police station and its officers currently train at two sites, Burtonwood Aerodrome and the Ministry of Defence centre at Holcombe Moor; on the expiry of these leases the GMP expects to build a new complex in Trafford Park which will simulate inner city conditions for counter insurgency operations.

The most senior officer reponsible for the TAG is the head of the Uniform Operational Support Group. On March 1st 1985 this was Superintendent John Hall. The Uniform Operational Support Group covers two other functions besides tactical aid, Emergency procedures and Operations Planning. One Chief Inspector heads the TAG units; beneath him are four Inspectors and seven sergeants[32].

On the night of March 1st. 1985, Superintendent Hall was outside the students union building with two other officers from 6.30pm. until 9.00pm. Only two units of twenty constables were used on the night and they were accompanied by two sergeants. These two TAG units were stationed at Longsight police stationed and it was there, in a small room, at 6.00pm, that they were briefed upon the operation.

The difference between TAG training and that of ordinary police officers, apart from its emphasis upon weapons and military strategy, is its concentration upon team work. Special military and policing teams which train and work together in different areas develop an esprit de corps and an elite view of their work. The emphasis upon fitness, technology, physical force and weapons training, together with the force wide powers these teams are given, lends them a position of isolation from the everyday policing practices of the rest of the force. They return to ordinary policing duties on the streets equipped with a military siege mentality.

Since their use against the National Graphical Association at Warrington, during the miners' strike and during various inner city disturbances throughout the country, these special para-military units have come under considerable criticism. The major concern, even from the liberal middle class, is that they are begining to resemble a standing army, that they inevitably feel themselves to be above the law and that they are a nacent force within a force.

Similar criticisms centred upon lack of accountability have already been aired in respect of the plain clothes special squads. Since their inception in the latter part of the nineteenth century, the detective police have been constantly criticised for acting like an army of spies, while mingling unaccountably with the civilian population. The Metropolitan Police detectives, especially, have always been considered prone to the development of less accountable and more autonomous political or criminal hegemony within the broader force. This general and abstract fear has proved to be justified time and time again. Since 1969, major corruption scandals have been exposed in the Flying Squad, the Porn Squad, the Vice Squad, the Fraud Squad, the Drugs Squad and most recently in the Robbery Squad[33].

There is a general rule of thunb which can be applied to corruption in the special squads; because they are visibly less accountable; because they come into contact with large quantities of illicit money; because they meet and mix with the most professional exponents of specialised crime and finally because the commerical organisation and the business ethic of the criminals involved is not actually opposed to the previaling ethic in the broader society, these squads begin themselves to organise profit within the areas of crime that they are meant to be policing. The Porn and Vice Squad corruption centred upon protection and dealing in pornography; Drug Squad corruption centred upon the re-sale of drugs and Robbery Squad corruption eventually led to the involvement of officers within firms of armed robbers. There seems some logic in the idea that, in a similar way, a squad whose raison d'etre is violence, who are trained to suppress riots, will end up rioting, or at least inflicting serious violence, themselves.

Problems began to develop in the special uniformed squads not long after the first of them, the Special Patrol Group, was set up in London in 1965. In 1973, officers from the SPG shot and killed two Asian protesters at the Indian High Commission in London. In 1979, the SPG attacked anti-nazi demonstrators in Southall, killing Blair Peach. A search of SPG lockers during the investigation of this case revealed illegal weapons ranging from crow bars to whips and coshes and at the home of one officer investigators found Nazi regalia. A similar raid of lockers at Greenheys Lane Police station in the wake of the Moss Side riots turned up, baseball bats and wooden staves.[34]

Trained as TAG officers are in small units, they develop a sense of protection towards each other which extends beyond the simple operational defence requirements of fellow officers. The enquiries into the Blair Peach killing in London were blocked at every turn by officers covering for each other. The same was true during the investigation of PSU officers involved in the assault upon four youths in the Holloway Road, London, in 1984[35]. Dealing as these officers do in violent and unpopular operations, they develop a sense of corporate protection which reaches into all their social relations. The fact that they frequently have to police unpopular laws further reinforces the conflict between them and the public.

At the sharp end of the State's military tactics to keep order, paramilitary police become the raison d'etre for policing itself; their hegemony and their tactics are solidly defended by the government and police strategists. Their simple use of military force appears, in the short term at least, to eradicate complex social deviancies. As this 'force' moves further away from the ordinary officers at the base of the policing function, all criticism of policing and tactics comes to centre upon them, as does all establishment defence of the use of 'reasonable' force. The boundaries of violence and lawlessness are gradually pushed further out and the nature of the whole force changes as a consequence.

The culture of these special units develops a combination of language and ritual which again earmarks them as elite shock troops. The TAG unit, like other such units, are given specially protective clothing which is much more than a uniform. The currency of their language is male and military. With some similarities to the plain clothes special squads their institutional language focuses upon sexual obscenities and derogatory sexual terms, especially directed against women. Their culture is essentially homophobic. By their culture and language they are united and almost continually in male company. That language which does not focus upon sexuality centres upon male violence and is a restricted language of threat and physical power. The Observer reported one TAG officer as summing up his professional work in the following way; 'If someone needs a thumping we'll give'em one.'[36]

In the operations of the special squads less and less attention is given to legal legitimacy. Their object in every operations is to resolve conflict by physical power rather than understand its source and act in accordance with reason or legal precedent. Officers in these units stand at the opposite end of a scale in social problem solving from the community police officers. They carry out orders without ever discussing their implications or being open to any dialogue with those whom they act against. Because of all these things, it could be said that they have a political function rather than a more traditional crime control function.

The TAG officers who assembled in Dover Street on March 1st.[37] and were briefed for the operation of seizing the steps, would have been trained as an armed and offensive force in all the military paraphernalia of hand to hand fighting with armed and unarmed civilians; shields, staves, flails, and in various forms of the martial arts[38]. The officers were accompanied on the night by alsation dogs and dog handlers. Beneath their nylon overjackets they wore protective clothing and their helmets were strengthened with special chin straps. A peculiarly large majority of these officers had full moustaches, which made later identification more difficult.

Another aspect of the TAG unit's sense of 'solidarity' and corporate defence worth noting is their determination to be unrecognisable. Since the inception of such units, attention has frequently been drawn to their missing 'collar numbers' (which are detachable from the new protective over jackets), the only means of identifying a particular police constable[39]. It is in relation to this small matter that we begin to see the parting of the ways between the statutory safeguards much talked of by senior officers and the tactics of junior officers in defence of their own jobs[40].

> People were being arrested for trying to take police officers' numbers, some of which were missing and almost all the remainder of which had been blacked out.
>
> ★
>
> It was at this time (approx. 8.30 pm.) when a friend and

> I asked one policeman whether they had been officially ordered to black out the last two numbers on their uniform when they charged the main steps at 7.15 pm. The policeman smiled mockingly and said that this would of course be illegal etc.
>
> ★
>
> One thing which I noticed at this stage was that they all had their numbers boot polished out.

The two TAG units from Longsight police station, which were in the vanguard of the assault upon the steps, were briefed by Inspector Smith from Bootle Street Police Station and it was he who commanded these two units and marched them towards the steps. During their briefing they were told that the Home Secretary was due to arrive at the building at 7.30 pm., and that they would move off when they received a communication from Superintendent Hall. They would march down Oxford Road and if it was necessary 'clear a passage way' up the steps. Officers arrived in Dover Street at about 6.30pm, in police coaches, Sherpa vans and militarised TAG carriers. As they awaited orders, they were stationed in Portland Street to the rear of the Holy Name Church. As well as the twenty TAG officers, there were between sixty and eighty PSU officers.

At the bottom of the union steps, Superintendent Hall, accompanied by a Sergeant from Withington Police Station and a Constable assessed the size of the demonstration and then communicated his orders to Inspector Smith. Smith led his men personally along Oxford Road and into the assault on the steps. He was the first officer to turn into the crowd. During a later court case he was to say; "As I led the officers up the steps I was met with resistance and I said, 'Excuse me, please, move to one side!' They conceded to my request at the bottom of the steps but by the time we reached the third and fourth steps it was obvious that they were not going to move."

Inspector Smith maintained during the court case that he led a serial of no more than twenty men, who formed the advance unit in the assault on the steps. The most charitable explanation of the discrepancy between Smiths' evidence and the eye witness reports of between sixty and one hundred officers is that while only two TAG units were briefed by Smith at Longsight, other PSU units were waiting in Portland Street to act as back up. When the order to clear the steps came, Smith was told that there were some 300 demonstrators, in light of this the other units fell in behind the TAG officers.

The senior officers at the demonstration had an on site briefing at 7.00 pm. when they made a decision about tactics. They stayed at the scene until 9.00pm, when they departed together in a coach.

The detectives who were present did not infiltrate themselves into the demonstration until the steps were almost full. There were at least ten of these officers who worked in pairs. They began arresting people as the steps were cleared and they continued until the Home Secretary had left the building. Unlike the uniformed TAG officers the detectives were not briefed on tactics or strategy, but they knew what was expected of them. They had probably volunteered for overtime duty. Their task was to break up the crowd from the inside using snatch squad techniques; and to point out to uniformed officers people whom they thought were a strategic problem. These officers went about their arrests in a bizarre and ad hoc manner. One student found himself captured when a plain clothes officer behind him snapped a metal clip onto his belt and dragged him away.

One plain clothes officer who later gave evidence in the court cases expressed surprise at the manner in which the steps had been cleared. He said that he would normally have expected a briefing meeting for that type of operation. Other detectives told the court that they were normally stationed at Longsight police station and had just attended for public order duty. Detectives Roberts and Manifold spoke of normally being on duty with the burglary squad. In relation to the burglary squad at Longsight, the Chief Constables report for 1985, makes an interesting point. It says that a new initiative involved the close cooperation of uniformed officers on surveillance duties with this squad.

The Greater Manchester Force had an Operational Support Group for cime and plain clothes officers as well as the Uniform Operational Support Group. The OSG (Crime) draws together officers from a number of different specialist squads to support general divisional operations. It is likely that the plain clothes officers present on March 1st came from this group and could have been taken from any of the following Squads which make up the group; Stolen Vehicles Squad, Commercial Fraud Squad, Drug Squad, Special Branch, or the Serious Crime Squad.

At the centre of the Operational Support Group (Crime), is the Force Criminal Intelligence section. All the officers who work in this section are operational detectives from various Squads, who collate, analyse and disseminate information on 'crime and associated matters'. This section is also responsible for a surveillance unit which is comprised mainly of trained uniformed officers. The OSG (Crime) is headed by a Detective Superintendent who in turn is responsible to a Chief Superintendent.

As Brittan finished his speech on March 1st, a number of officers entered the union building. Some made their way to the Serpent bar where they stood in front of the windows; others moved in to guard the stairways which Brittan came down. They briefly closed off all the entrances to the foyer while the Home Secretary moved through it and out onto the steps. It was this last group of officers, walking out of the union building just ahead of Sarah Hollis, who appear to have been responsible for one of the most violent arrests of the night; it was also most probably someone in this group who threw Sarah Hollis down the steps.

The cell vans for prisoners were parked just a little way down Oxford Road past the union building[41]. During the course of the evening these two vans appear to have delivered three groups of prisoners to Greenheys Lane and Longsight police station. Almost at the end of the evening, between 8.30pm and 9.00pm, after the Home Secretary had left and as the police tried to clear any remaining students off the pavement by pushing them up towards Rusholme, three of four violent arrests occurred.

Two of these arrests are of particular interests. Mark Sowden and David Pannell were both arrested between 8.30pm and 8.45pm. Both students were walked down the road, and in the temproary absence of both cell vans were placed in an unmarked red Ford Cortina police car. When the cell van arrived they were taken to Greenheys Lane police station. There was only one other mention of any saloon cars at the scene; in evidence at a later court case, Detective Sergeant Manifold told the court that he had written up his notes on the arrest of Sean Moor while sitting in a police car outside the Holy Name

Church. The relevance of a saloon car, and particularly a red Ford Cortina, will become clear later.

The two TAG units that Inspector Smith had briefed and which spearheaded the assualt on the steps, stayed on or around the steps and wandered in and out of the building until they finished their duty at 9.00pm. In the main, officers did not escort prisoners to their police stations but gave prisoners names to cell van drivers and then followed up with their processing after they had finished duty. Most of the officers, even those from Salford, first went back to their stations with the remainder of their units, before making their way to the cells at either Greenheys Lane or Longsight.

At the police stations, none of the prisoners were allowed a phone call and all were fingerprinted and photographed. Some were kept in custody a considerable length of time; until two or three in the morning. Others claim to have been abused and treated aggressively, especially at Greenheys Lane.

Chapter Four

Gutter Culture

"Understand this lad. You can't get away with cheek. Kids nowadays treat any kind of authority as a challenge. We'll challenge you. If you oppose me in my duty, I'll kick those teeth through the back of your head. Is that clear?"

Joe Orton's uncompromisingly sadistic detective Truscott in the play **Loot.**

This book is centrally about a conspiracy which was born and had its roots in the policing of the Leon Brittan demonstration. Because its beginnings appear so inauspicious, and because its rationale is difficult to understand from a position outside the police force, it is necessary to look at the behaviour of the police on that night, not simply in terms of bald events but culturally and politically. It is necessary as well to understand a little about their obsessive secrecy and their constant denial that a specific police culture exists.[42] It is in fact only by trying to understand how the police behave inside their own closed institution that we can understand their need for a conspiracy and the power they use to organise it.

The Home Secretary is the national head of the police. He is not simply a politician of primary importance within the State, he is also a manager of State forces. The police more than any other agency in our present society are the manifestation of coercive State power, a power which is exerted in direct conflict with large parts of the population on the streets and at the point of production.

However, despite the apparent political and cultural hegemony between State managers and their agents, there are divergent and conflicting interests involved for both groups. The State has to ensure the safety and purity of its important personages, creating the space and the freedom for them to move through the world undefiled. Individual police officers, on the other hand, while also having to project this ultimate 'good' publically, have other quite personal objectives and considerations.

The relationship between the State's objectives and the more personal objectives of the police constable is cultural as well as structural. Those of the constables on March 1st, were two fold. The structural objectives came within their terms of employment; to clear the union steps of students and take all the necessary measures to facilitate the entry and exit of the Home Secretary. They were briefed upon this set of objectives by their line management.

What of the second set of objectives? In part these involved ensuring that after they had done their job they did not fall victim to complaint; a complaint which would be levelled *against them personally,* not their management. They had to guard their backs and ensure that they survived and kept their jobs. Within a closed institution like the police force, this was not a problem that each officer had to be specifically aware of individually; the force was with them.

Another part of their objective was immensely more personal and ideological, imposing discipline upon a group of people whose aims, ambitions and general identity they saw as being in conflict with their own. To the average para-military officer, with a lower middle class or non-unionised working class background and lumpen ideology, students present a real threat; even more so, socialist students. Conjoined with this generic group, in the minds of many police officers, are black people, feminists, supporters of all kinds of international campaigns, communists, homosexuals, anarchists and a general slag of people living a soft option at the expense of the tax-payer. It is these people who have all the chances, the good fortune of background and grants, who should be working rather than demonstrating. Such people are permissive, dirty and disorganised and they do not believe in the authority of the State. The personal objective for some TAG officers then, could have been to manifest, through violence and the imposition of order, the power of their own ideology.

There are points at which the structural objectives of the force as a whole overlap with the more personal objectives of individual officers. Following what happened on the steps, other 'force considerations' had to be taken into account. Nationally the use of para-military tactics has come under close scrutiny and criticism. Within the Greater Manchester police force itself, the efficiency and tactical usefulness of the TAG units is gauged by reports from divisional commanders to force senior officers. Within any division, TAG officers have to justify themselves in terms of their efficiency. It is therefore within their interests to pursue a 'damage limitation' strategy after an operation like that of March 1st.

If the objectives of the individual officers had been simply to carry out their orders one would imagine that the distastful job would have been done quickly and quietly and that officers would then have shown concern for their victims. They would have evinced a view of 'being in the middle' or 'only doing their jobs.' This is not what happened; officers appeared to act with deep seated ideological intent and were too drugged on violence and institutionalised power to return to anything vaguely resembling sympathetic human behaviour.

Most of the statements written by students three days after they had been attacked were full of integrity. But while they almost all contained details of the physical struggle that took place, relatively few concentrated upon the culture and the ideology expressed by the police. We have looked at the physical violence acted out by the police that night, and structurally at their composition; let us look now, picking through those statements, at the ideology and culture which officers expressed.

> I heard police officers say: ''Lets get in there lads.'' I heard one officer say, ''We can take the law into our own hands.'' Two police officers did a bit of play acting for our benefit:
>
> *First officer:* ''Do you want to start something with me?''
> *Second officer:* ''That's provocation.''
> *First officer:* ''You stand up in court and say that.''

This is a subconscious language of power, spoken before a defenceless group. As during the miners strike this culture is also linked to economic advantage; miners on strike were on subsistence levels of income, students' grants are not much more. Police officers use these facts to drive home the reality of their position in the State heirarchy and the power which accompanies it:

> I saw one person arrested for trying to cross the road. One officer said loudly, ''I'm on time and a third,'' another answered even more loudly, ''I'm on time and a half.''

Para-military police officers hate young middle class women almost as vehemently as they hate working class and black women.

Women on the steps became particular targets of police violence when a number of them were thrown by their hair down the steps. This strategic response in clearing the steps is reflected at a much deeper ideological level in the following reports:

> I was standing on the pavement searching for a friend in the crowd, to the right of the steps. A policeman walked up to me and blocked my way. He said sneeringly; "Have you anything you wanted to say to me scum?" I suspected that this was provocation so I walked round him.
>
> ★
>
> I heard many comments passed about the nature of the women. The police officers called them 'whores' and said things like, "I wouldn't sleep with you if I was paid." A whole series of comments were issued by police officers.
>
> ★
>
> I heard things like "Come on, you stupid bitch, let's be having you" and "Come on you fucking whore."

Another obvious manifestation of personal and ideological power is the threat of arbitrary arrest and the casual use of assumed arbitrary powers:

> I heard a policeman say; "Come on, we need a few more arrests, our van isn't full yet."
>
> ★
>
> Several times, I tried to enter the union after the police had cleared the steps. At first, the policeman on the opposite side of the road refused to let me pass, although I explained that I wanted to enter the building to see a group who were performing that night. The officer had decided that no one was to enter the building unless attending the meeting; eventually I and my friend were allowed to cross the road. As I entered the building, my friend was stopped as he was only carrying his NUS card and not his library card. We then returned

to Whitworth Park to collect his library card, then went back to the union. Once again, the police would not let us pass, making these decisions as individuals although we explained that I had already entered the building once.

A large part of police culture is acted out simply through verbal intimidation and the cold blooded threat of violence or retribution:

> I was first aware of this officer when he hit the lad standing next to me, knocking off and breaking his glasses. A short while later he was attempting to hold people in their position by shoving the heel of his hand into their face. When he did this to me, I made the mistake of putting my arm in front of my face. Immediately, both he and his brother officer grabbed me by the throat and I was warned *"Don't even think of it,"*
>
> ★
>
> "Come on lads get your truncheons out, a few of these want splinters in their heads."
>
> ★
>
> I remember one policeman at that point saying, "Some heads are going to get kicked in," and another student pushed forward and said, "What's your number, show me your number," and he made a great show of pushing his shoulder forward and saying, "There it is, take it and see what good it will do you."

These verbal threats have much greater power when they are accompanied by actual physical violence and especially when they are uttered within the frightening isolation of the police station;

> At the police station, I was molested by one of the policemen who in the course of my search called me 'dick-head' for refusing to give up my shoes. And when I protested about the way that he escorted me back to the cell, which was with violence, he punched me in the stomach saying something

> to the effect of "You should know who you are dealing with." On the second occasion that I was taken from the cell to be questioned, I was abused, hit on the head, punched in the back and thrown into the cell. The police officer followed me into the cell and threatened me, saying, "You shouldn't mess with the police."

One of the first imperatives of police culture during any attack, dictates that the incident is 'depublicised.' All symbolic forms of public announcement about what people are protesting against, or of what the police have done to achieve their objective have to be destroyed or at least contained.

> "Get the banners," I heard one policeman yell.
>
> ★
>
> I saw one officer manically smashing up placards.

Linked to this imperative and the need for officers to survive and protect their jobs in the light of any complaints or court cases, is the need to obstruct anyone who is taking photographs.

> I then witnessed a male student being punched on the side of the head. When another student, whom I did not know, attempted to photograph the officer in question, his camera was taken from him. When asked why, the response was, "He's camera shy."
>
> ★
>
> One young woman was moved to suggest that the officer might have been born out of wedlock. In answer to this he grabbed her by the hair and pulled her out of the crowd to hand her over to two other officers twice her size; they dragged her away. Another officer saw the lad next to me about to take a photograph so he grabbed his camera and threw it on the ground, then he grabbed him by the throat and told him to "Fuck off."

★

> Another woman told me that she had been taking photographs of people being arrested and was told by a policeman to stop doing this, or he would "have her."

Some of the students, spurred on either by naïvete or pure anger, continued against all odds to press for their rights. The student below fought a small unsuccessfull guerilla campaign, in an attempt to identify one particular officer.

> As police officers leading the attack neared the union doors, a constable, identifiable at the time by his lacking a helmet, struck me, fist clenched, on the side of the head. I ended up at the bottom of the steps. The officer who had struck me was now above me on the steps, our positions were reversed, he now had absolutely no need to resort to any physical action, he could have asked me to leave the steps as other P.C.'s were doing. However, he punched me twice on the left shoulder. As we waited for Brittan, I stood on the edge of the police cordon on the north side of the steps. I was able to spot the officer in question from a distance, but could not read his number. I pointed him out to various bystanders and policemen in the cordon. He donned a strapless helmet but was still identifiable to me. I pointed directly at him, he stared back. I stressed the fact that he had no strap on his helmet to those around me as I tried to read his number. A constable in the cordon went up the steps and spoke to a P.C. who in turn spoke to the one who had punched me. Within minutes, a helmet with a strap was brought up to him by a constable who appeared from the Oxford Road side. I regarded this as a deliberate ploy to prevent me from confirming an identity later. After Brittan had entered the Union I managed to walk around the cordon and approach an officer on the pavement. He was reasonable though glib until I spotted my attacker in the act of savagely dragging away a protester along with several other P.C.s. As I tried to point him out, the officer at once told me to

> go home and threatened me with arrest. In my opinion, he blatantly ignored my attempt to make an official complaint.

The policing of the student demonstration on March 1st, presents us with a micorcosm of police behaviour and culture. Threads of this culture, as different from established structural orders, were to run through the case of harassment for over a year following the demonstration.

We can see that from a structural point of view the demonstration was policed in a para-military manner with some efficiency. This is the contemporary method of policing dissent and it is an extension of this kind of policing that we will all have to face in the future.

From the point of view of police culture we see something which is uglier and more sinister. The para-military machine is not composed of smaller unit machines which respond with professional exactitute but of officers who, in the majority have a right wing lumpen ideology. These officers on the one hand act out the orders of their senior officers, but on the other are bound together in the lower ranks with their own esprit de corps, their own personal and political objectives and their own sense of hegemonous protection. *In order to enforce the law the police establishment has to employ constables in its service who break the law continually, and in their turn, these officers have to defend themselves against people who use the law to bring them to account.*

A brief examination of the component parts of police culture that we have described and which is well documented elswhere[43], will confirm its ideological shape. Officers express a personal ideology which is rooted in male violence; which propounds a detestation of independent or intelligent women; which is racist; which is publicaly homophobic; which has a profound mistrust of intelligence and intellectualism; which is anti-socialist; which believes in the authority of the State above all other institutions; which is hierachical and based upon discipline and orders rather than debate; which thrives upon secrecy and resents criticism of any kind, while destroying any public symbolism of its illegality or deviance. Broadly speaking this is the culture and the ideology of fascism.

The State in our society does not espouse fascism as its ideology but an authoritarianism which demands a high degree of order and control. However, fascist ideology at the base of the police force serves the purpose of the State and the structural requirements of senior officers.

What was to unfold in Manchester after March 1st shows clearly how the culture and the structure of repression has developed in countries with authoritarian regimes, such as those of Latin America. There, the base of the policing agencies have detached themselves from the guiding structures and become a 'force within a force'. This detachment and the right wing ideology which accompanies it provide a foundation for police vigilantism.

Missing Presumed Stolen

Steven Shaw's first year at Manchester University had been spent in student accommodation. But there was something claustrophobic about the student ghetto and he decided to look for a place to live beyond Manchester centre, where the dark and solid brick buildings gave way to fields and farms. He was fortunate in finding a flat in a large converted farm house on the very edge of the country.

The accommodation was excellent although his relationship with his landlord and landlady, who lived in the ajoining house was, on occasion, strained. Over the last year there had been a number of incidents which, he believed, had their roots in the political or personal differences between himself and his landlords. On one occasion he had been asked to remove a badge which he wore in support of the miners when he entered their house.

Steve's first day back at the university after the demonstration was eventful. Once back amongst his friends, he realised that the assault on the students the Friday before had been an important policing event. Attending a previously planned meeting about his thesis with the head of the Manchester City Council Police Monitoring Unit[44], that Monday, the discussion had inevitably turned to the demonstration. Steve Wright, the head of the unit, offered to give the students any help they wanted in writing up and investigating the way that the police had behaved.

After the meeting Steve left the Town Hall and drove to the Students Union where an ad hoc meeting was being held at one thirty. Before the meeting began he spent time talking to other students about issues to be raised. There was the necessary work to be done on the cases of those who had been arrested; statements had to be taken, witnesses found and a collective defence line resolved. There was also the important issue of the role that the Students' Union executive had played on the night; what had been the content of meetings and discussions that had taken place between union officers and the police? Why had executive members and security staff locked the doors at the top of the steps?

The meeting took place in the main debating hall and was attended by about 150 students. One student organiser sat at the front on the edge of the stage and chaired the meeting. Within five minutes of its beginning, a show of union cards was asked for, and on this, one older man left the hall. A number of statements were gathered by student activists at the meeting and put together with those which had been taken earlier in the day. Photographs were also handed over to the students.

Towards the end of the meeting, Steve stood up and told students about his conversation earlier that day with Steve Wright. There was evident scepticism amongst some students about the role of the Labour controlled City Council, but the majority of the meeting wanted all the statements and photographs to be shown to the Monitoring Unit staff. The meeting delegated three people to accompany Steve to a meeting in the unit.

This meeting took place in the late afternoon with a secretary taking notes. Having read the statements, Steve Wright was even more convinced that the City Council should assist the students.

Steven Shaw left the meeting with the only collection of evidence about the behaviour of the police on that night; he had been instructed by the defence meeting not to leave it with the Monitoring Unit. Driving back to the University from the city centre he decided that it would be most secure in the safe at the students' union. On reaching the union, he handed over the documents to the union manager who put them in the safe.

Steve was preoccupied with the problems that had been thrown up by the police attack on the students. None of the activists at the university had faced the difficulties of such a large defence campaign before. Should the police complaints system be used? Could a more independent inquiry be set up, such as the one that Steve Wright was beginning to talk about?

At seven thirty, after more discussion with friends, Steve left the union and went to meet a friend who was visiting Manchester. They drove back to Steve's flat where they spent the evening talking about his thesis, the demonstration and politics in general. His friend wanted to attend the Jackie Berkeley trial, Steve agreed to accompany him the following morning.

The mornings were quiet and pleasant in the small village. Steve and his friend drove down the long hill road between dry stone walls into the outskirst of Oldham and then on into the city. At Crown Square, a new court complex, they spoke to the continuous picket which had attended the Berkeley trial and Steve's friend went into the public gallery. It was on the steps of the court that Steve remembered that he wouldn't be going back to the flat that night and that he had forgotton a number of things.

The drive back out to Oldham would take half an hour; he could either go now or at the end of the day. He decided to go back straight away, there would be little traffic, and anyway, he had some time to spare before an appointment with his tutor. As he walked back to his car he thought about Jackie Berkeley; the strain which the trial must have put on her. He wondered momentarily how capable he would be of withstanding such a strain.

The wide Oldhan Road stretches North East out of Manchester, bringing relief from the architectural clutter of the centre. On either side reclaimed industrial land is dotted with closed and disused shops and bulky old mill buildings. On the edge of Oldham the scene begins to resemble industrial villages. Then you are in the country. Hard stone walls dissect dark green fields. Nothing here has escaped from its industrial heritage, this is not the flower and farm country of Kent, or the prettified conserve of the Cotswolds. The dry stone walls of this countryside are impregnated with the soot from a thousand mills and chimneys.

Waterhead is a trickle of run down conurbation on the edge of Oldham. The fields beyond the main road are littered with stone farm houses and outhouse buildings. To reach 'Top of the Meadow Farm', Steve turned left off the main road and climbed a long grey road between hedges and banks. The road was narrow and intermittently he could see the house perched on the side of the hill. About fifty yards from his destination, he saw a stationary white Sherpa police van.

He concentrated on the road and drove past the empty van cautiously, noticing the logo of the Greater Manchester Police on the side.

At the top of the road, there was a small hamlet of houses and farm buildings. Here the road ended and a dusty earthen yellow track began. 'Top of the Meadow Farm' was one of the last buildings before the end of the road. A large well kept stone farm house with some additions, and with a strip of well kept garden at the front, it looked out from the side of the hill. The house was built on a slope and the door to Steve's flat was at the rear, down a gravel path, hemmed in on one side by a dry stone wall, on the other by the house itself.

The journey had taken about half an hour and it was now ten forty five; he drove the car through the stone gates and parked on the pale gravel moon at the front. The sight of the police van had made him a little apprehensive; but why should it? He walked round the side of the house and up the narrow path at the back. Before he reached the door he could see that there was something wrong.

The door was ajar with a thin line of darkness between itself and the frame. Closer now, he could see what looked like an indentation two thirds of the way up the door near the frame, as if someone had thrown their shoulder against it. Above the indentation there seemed to be a slight crack in the hardboard. He became frightened; perhaps there was still someone in the flat. He was acutely aware of the isolation and the silence of the country that surrounded him. He pushed the door open gently. Looking down he could see that the metal hasp which took the tongue of the lock was bent and pushed out.

Inside the flat he looked around, tentatively at first, then more boldly. He took a broom from beside the door and waved it about uncommitedly inside cuboards and under the bed. There was no one there. He stood up and began to take stock of the flat. Nothing seemed disturbed, there was no mess. His record player and radio were still there. He looked again towards the door and saw the flakes of paint on the floor; the flat had definitely been broken into, but what had been stolen?

He looked on the shelves almost opposite the door and then he saw clearly. Two large box files which had lain on their side, labelled 'POLICE TECHNOLOGY AND SURVEILLANCE', and which had contained material for his thesis, were no longer there. He looked quickly through other papers, books and reports but nothing else was missing. Even then, he could think of no reason why anyone would would want to steal his thesis material.

He found a screw driver and unscrewed the hasp from the door frame; by bashing it on the stones outside, he was able to straighten it out. With some difficulty he screwed it back and pulled the door hard into the frame; it didn't seem to be badly damaged. He locked it again. He felt very confused, but his overriding feeling was that he wanted to get away from this isolated place as quickly as possible. He knocked on the front door of his landlord's house and when there was no reply he called at the house which overlooked his flat at the back. He got no answer there either and decided to drive back into town.

He drove nervously down the hill road and saw from the top that the white police Sherpa had gone. He had only left the flat two hours ago, how had the burglars known that he wasn't in. And again the question came to his mind, who would want to break into his flat and steal his thesis material.

Chapter Five

The Trials of Being a Student

"What do you know about this business?" The King said to Alice.
"Nothing," said Alice.
"Nothing whatever?" persisted the King.
"Nothing whatever," said Alice.
"That's very important," the King said, turning to the jury.

Lewis Carroll: Alice in Wonderland

The modern authoritarian State is offended by minorities; pluralism, tolerance and liberality only survive when there is an excess of profit. But seen as even more offensive are those who organise with a different and alternative culture, those whose way of life displays different social relations from those legitimised by the State. Order can only be imposed efficiently upon those who behave in a uniform way and believe the same things to be true. The most fundamental struggle for the State in late industrial society was the struggle against the collectivity and community which grew up in the nineteenth century; a similarity of feeling and experience based upon production. Now, in the post-industrial era, new communities rise quickly as the old communities are broken up, no longer based upon production they carry the flags of a myriad new and different feelings towards the world.

To destroy autonomous minorities whose social relations are different, the State relies primarily upon the new means of production which like the factory system are inherently a new means of control. The new means of production are diffuse and sometimes invisible. The new worker has a dialogue only with a screen or button, with electronically produced symbols which flicker and die before the eyes. The collective power of a socialised workforce is no longer required by those who control production, fewer and more separate workers are needed. This transfer from one mode of production to another is creating a massive surplus population. These people linger on the threshold of economic life. They mill about, beginning again to feel, wanting to be involved, wishing to create. They see within their grasp a world of leisure where the necessary work is done by machines.

Rather than being released from the penury of enforced work to enjoy a new humanity, they become the victims of enforced leisure with no control over their lives. The valueless individuals of the post industrial society, trying without resources to find a new reason for existence, beaten and berated, are pushed and prodded to get on their bikes and look for work. In the absence of work, this new and devalued class is a continual threat to the order and the stability of the State. This is the new criminal estate, but the peverse logic of capitalism determines that you cannot be criminal unless you break the law. New laws are created, which the valueless are bound to break because they proscribe their very existence.

In 1984, some time before the miners' strike began, a Green paper on Public Order was drafted. This Public Order Bill, as it is now, is the first organisation of *general rules* drafted by the State in Britain, to control those who are not disciplined by the new means of production and, to inhibit their social relations.

The Bill is characterised by a determination to break up any gathering which might interfere with the smooth running of production, exchange and consumption. To stop pickets, boycotts, occupations, work place meetings or demonstrations at places of work or in areas of consumption such as shopping centres. It articulates a determination to break up any gathering which by virtue of its internal social relations, poses a threat to the political order of the State; groups who smoke cannabis; travellers and gypsies; hippies and festival goers; women at Greenham Common; groups of gay men and lesbian women; organised groups who demand work.

This assault upon community and feeling is not simply physical, it is also spatial. The Public Order Bill is also characterised by the extension of State contol from public into private space. From control of the streets, to the control of public meetings held in halls, finally to the control of domestic space. Under the Public Order Bill the police will be able to break up meetings inside people's homes. Ultimately the order of the State reaches beyond private space into the mind and the body, ordering the very identity of the human individual.

But not only are gatherings assaulted and broken up, new and more frightening means are employed by the State to do this and a new type of police force is organised to carry out this task. In the public domain, they are equipped like an army with an array of lethal weapons and the powers to use them. In the private domain, spies, informers and plain clothes detectives are all invested with new powers to reach deep into the substance of the individual's life.

If it is the case that the change in the means of production gives a green light to the State to begin disbanding communities, it is also the case that there is no obvious or readily graspable rational in the public mind for this new rule of order. Contemporary reasons have to be invented and publicly manifest. There have to be symbolic hooks upon which to hang new laws and a new ideology of order. Students are a good anvil for the hammer of this new order; by their very nature they do not appear to produce and the liberal structure of the institutions of learning allows them the space to develop life styles which are different. And if it is the case that they do not much feel like causing trouble, then trouble can be thrust upon them. In March 1985, with the miners' strike almost at an end and the Public Order Bill drifting out of its visible context, new ways had to be found of propagandising the new rule of order.

★★★

The court cases for the arrested students began in early April, five weeks after the demonstration. For some students, their trial was the end of the incident which had begun on the steps. Many of them must have been thankful to get their cases over. They did what they could to work collectively with other arrested students, but at the end of the day, they wanted to put the matter behind them and get on with their work.

If students were shocked and affected by the violence shown by the police when they attacked the demonstration on the steps, many of them were to be much more shocked by the nature of the evidence given against them in court. At trial, the breaking up of the demonstration had been retrospectively deemed a public order situation. Consequently it seemed to matter little to some of the magistrates *who had created* the disorder or whether it had taken place in a 'private' or a 'public' place.[45]

As the nature of the State changes so does the criminal law. The previous more refined rules of custody, interrogation and evidence, together with the statutes which govern the actual apprehension of offenders, are swept aside and replaced by a self generated police rule of thumb which is general in the extreme. In the period before new laws are framed to suit the new social order, while the law is in a state of flux, the police themselves make the law and continually validate their own power by selecting those they arrest and the evidence they give against them, on the simple basis of political expediency.

When the police bring their public order offender and their evidence before the court, they are forced to pay some respect to the previous heritage of legal rules. To do this they sometimes manufacture crimes committed against them by the defendant and evidence to back up their allegations. Somehow it has to appear that the arrested person has infringed a law. On March 1st, outside the Students' Union building, there was only one group of people breaking the law and that was the police. It was they who created a public disturbance , it was they who created an affray, it was they who committed offences of common assault and actual bodily harm. The students were committing an offence but it was one which had not at that time nor has yet been enshrined in statute; they were gathering together to demonstrate their disagreement with a minister of the government and to display a set of values and social relations which were in opposition to those propagated by the State and the police.

There were thirty eight people arrested on the night, but only thirty three of these were charged. The majority of the charges, twenty three, were under section 5 of the Public Order Act 1936.[46] Others were for obstructing the police, obstructing the highway and assaulting police officers. During the trials, there were attempts by defence solicitors to explain the context of the demonstration and to point out to the bench that the police had moved in on the crowd without any warning. The police, on the other hand, placed the onus of initiating the disturbances upon the students. In a number of cases this involved offering the most amazing stories. Of those charged, one pleaded guilty and nineteen were convicted, the remaining fourteen being found not guilty. The sentences imposed included conditional discharge, fines, and in one case fourteen days imprisonment.[47]

Name	Charge	Taken To	Defendant's Evidence	Sentence	Time of Arrest
Nigel Spencer	Breach of Peace			Dismissed	
Mark Sowden	Theft of PO. Helmet	Greenheys		Dismissed	8.20pm
Chris Simpson	Threatening Behaviour			12 mnth.Cond. Dis. £25 costs.	
Andrew Buttress	Assaulting PO. Obstruction of PO			£100 fine £10 costs	7.20pm
Stephen Ryden				£60 fine £10 costs	
David Pannel	Assault of a PO	Greenheys		£100 fine	9.10pm
Nicholas Cotter	Breach of the Peace	Longsight		12 months Con. Dis. £25 costs	8.15pm.
Kevin Thrope	Obstruction	Longsight	Thrown down steps face down, dragged by hair	Unconditional Discharge	7.30pm
Howard Barber	Obstruction		Elbowed in face	Dismissed	7.30pm
Paul Banham	Obstruction of PO	Longsight		£50 fine £20 costs	7.45pm
David Brown	Disorderly Behaviour	Greenheys	Abusive remarks about homosexuality	Dismissed	9.15pm.
Donald Forder	Obstruction	Longsight		Dismissed	
Charles Alcock	Threatening Behaviour	Greenheys	Bloodied nose, injured head	Dismissed	9.15pm.
Justin Byrne	Obstruction of PO	Longsight		12 months. Cond. Dis. £20 costs	7.45pm.
Gail Day	Threatening Behaviour	Longsight	Violent arrest	2yrs. Cond. Dis. £30 costs.	7.40pm
Peter Forbes	Obstruction	Longsight	Dragged by hair	Cond. Discharge	8.00pm
Martin Ives	Breach of Peace			£40 fine £20 costs	7.20pm.

Name	Charge	Taken To	Defendant's Evidence	Sentence	Time of Arrest
Anna Wildsmith	Threatening Behaviour			12 months. Cond. Dis. £35 costs	7.55pm
Kieron Wardell	Assault PO Threat. Beh.	Longsight		£75 fine, £50 cost	7.55pm
Elizabeth Marks	Obstructing PO	Longsight		12 months. Cond. Dis. £50 costs.	7.55pm
Marcus Powells	Breach of Peace	Longsight		12 months. Cond. Dis. £12 costs	
Paul Philips	Obstruction	Longsight	Abusive language, grabbed from crowd, dragged backwards	Dismissed	7.30pm.
Duncan Staff	Breach of Peace		Thrown down steps Hit in face	Dismissed	8.15pm
Farid Kawar	Obstructing PC	Greenheys		Dismissed	8.30pm app
Richard Lumb	Obstruction PC		Violent arrest	Dismissed Cost awarded	9.15pm
Sean Moore	Breach of peace	Longsight	PC broke glasses Abused and threatened	Dismissed Cost awarded	9.15pm app
Mark Ormrod	Threatening Behaviour			£50 fine £25 costs	
Gary Todd	Threatening Behaviour	Longsight	Thrown down steps, banged head	Unconditional Discharged £25 cost	8.10pm.
John Traynor	Threatening Behaviour	Longsight		14 days Imprisonment	7.40pm.
William Philips	Obstruction	Longsight	Dragged backwards, punched, Glasses broken	Dismissed	
Simon Ryan	Breach of Peace	Longsight	Pulled from crowd, dragged to van	Dismissed	
Andrew Jones	Obstruction	Longsight	Pulled down steps by hair.	Dismissed	7.50pm.
Iqbal Butt	Breach of the Peace			Dismissed	

As in many 'Public Order' situations, defendants were lost during the processing and ended up at trial being 'arrested' by officers whom they had never seen before. Some students claimed Officers had swapped and bartered arrested individuals on the basis of 'sparebodies'. Officers came to court prepared to say that they had formally arrested people when they had done nothing of the sort. A number of defendants claimed that obscenities, bizarre political chants and expressions about police fascism as well as verbal admissions supposedly made during interviews in the police station bore no relationship to what they had said. While it appeared to many students that some police officers treated the court cases as a utilitarian game by which they justified their own powers, to the students they were more serious.

The cases began on the 9th April and continued with regularity until the end of May. The most punitive sentence was against a young man called John Traynor. He was awarded fourteen days imprisonment because he had raised his arms and 'runaround' at the very moment that the Home Secretary was being shuffled up the steps by his honour guard. His body, lost in the melee of constables and Special Branch Officers, did not provide a target of any vulnerability. In fact every part of him except for the very top of his balding head was obscured. However, to the Magistrate, the symbolic threat appears to have been there.

When an impressive video film showing was organised by the prosecution in Traynor's case, neither the defence, nor the prosecution, nor for that matter anyone in the court, could actually see Traynor or anyone else acting in a threatening manner in the immediate vicinity of the Home Secretary.

In October 1985, seven cases went to Appeal. They were heard by Judge Arthur Prestt Q.C., Recorder of Manchester, and although four cases, including that of Traynor, were dismissed, three were upheld.

During the hearings, the Judge accused two officers of lying when they claimed to have made notes together following the arrest of one student. The truth was, he said, that the notes were made up by one P.C. when his colleague was not even in the police station. "Where one finds a deception practiced on the lower court, evidence given by police officers which was false, then no court can safely rely upon the evidence given by the same witnesses in the same case.'' The students version of events was accepted and his appeal against conviction for obstructing the highway allowed.

In the case of Elizabeth Marks, Prestt reserved some caustic remarks with respect to the evidence given at trial by two of the plain clothes detectives.

> This court does not regard the evidence of P.C. O'Connor or P.C. Walshe as satisfactory, or as evidence on which this court can properly rely. O'Connor made conflicting statements which did not agree with the arresting officer. We have little doubt that the marked inconsistencies between the two statements made by O'Connor can be explained by his having deliberately or unwittingly tailored his evidence to bring it in line with what he knew or believed would be the evidence of the arresting officers.
>
> In relation to W.P.C. Walshe (a plain clothes police woman), she countersigned O'Connor's notebook and made a witness statement on the 20th. March. That witness statement is nothing more than a parrot duplication of O'Connor's statement. They were both made at the same time. It is inconsistent with the arresting officer's statment and is demonstrably inaccurate.

It is not surprising that Judge Prestt reserved these remarks for a case involving plain clothes detectives. While uniformed constables might appear to have a real role in such 'Public Order' situations, the role of plain clothes detectives appears less plausible, possibly entailing snatching people, breaking up the crowd and acting as agents provocateurs. Undercover within the crowd, they are nor surrounded by other officers who can witness their arrests and then their statements. Giving evidence in other court cases, two plain clothes officers told the court that they had made three separate arrests within the space of ten minutes. It would be very difficult to argue that these arrest could have had any proper procedural foundation, and even more difficult to argue that the officers concerned could have written proper notes of the arrests.

The function of plain clothes officers in crowds or demonstrations is quite simply a 'para-military' function and has nothing to do with normal criminal policing practices. Even for plain clothes detectives working on criminal cases, the law has always been ambivalent about the fine dividing line between participation in the commission of offences and inactive surveillance. That at least ten plain clothes detectives were deployed inside the demonstration outside the union building, makes them in effect a substantial part of the demonstration, and it could be argued participants. It is also a reflection of the scale and priorities of resources given by the Greater Manchester Police to 'subversion' as against 'crime'. With crime clear-up rates so abysmally low in Manchester and everywhere else, it is nothing short of negligence to deploy ten detectives from serious crime squads in a small and disorganised student protest.

Plain clothes officers act without any of the constraints of uniformed officers. We have discussed how even the uniformed officers had done everything possible to obstruct their identification; plain clothes officers did not have to resort to any such tactics. Even now, we know only of those plain clothes officers there on the night who gave evidence in court. The deployment of plain clothes officers in such numbers and such circumstances begins to form a prerequisite condition, even at the start of this case, for the development of the unaccountable and rogue 'hit squads' which later became its salient feature.

On March 1st, these detectives were disguised as students; they had not attended any briefing and were answerable to no specific senior officer. They did not declare themselves before physically apprehending anyone. If, at the end of the day, it is just possible to find out the names, rank and station of the uniformed officers who were present on the night, it is simply impossible to find out who was deployed in plain clothes. As the case continued, it became crucially important to be able to name and have access to those detectives who were employed on the night.

PART TWO

THE FORCE WITHIN A FORCE

"Curioser and curioser!" cried Alice.

Lewis Caroll: Alice in Wonderland

The question of whether we treat some other individual as a policeman or as a criminal will depend not on the facts of the case but what we believe to be the case with regard to the legitimacy of the situation.

Edmund Leach: Custom, Law and Terrorist Violence

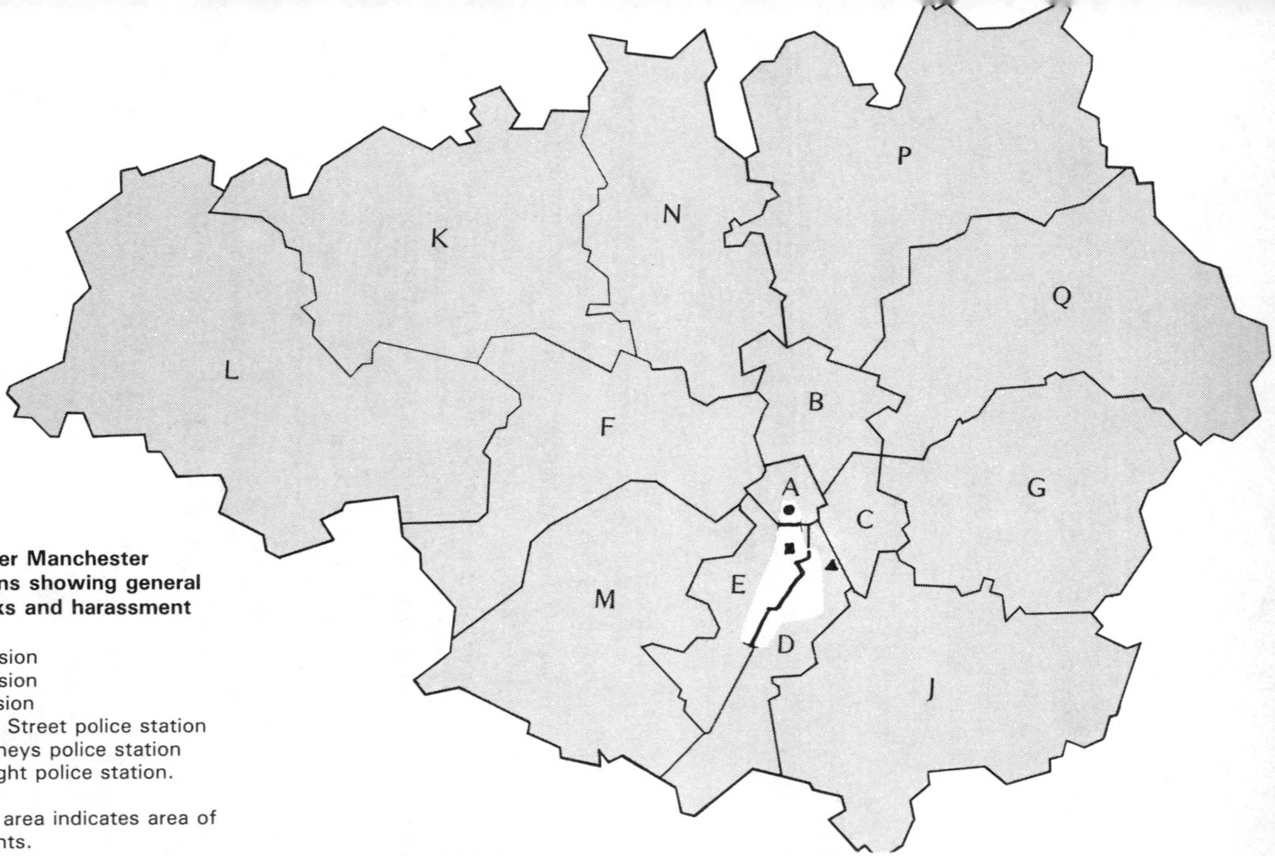

Map of Greater Manchester police Divisions showing general area of attacks and harassment

A	A Division
D	D Division
E	E Division
●	Bootle Street police station
■	Greenheys police station
▲	longsight police station.

White area indicates area of incidents.

Two Ways of Seeing

> *Don't forget, always let me know straight away if you need anything because I know people everywhere. Because I'm in a little firm in a firm. Don't matter where, anywhere in London I can get on the phone to someone I know I can trust, that talks the same as me. And if he's not the the right person that can do it, he'll know the person that can. All right?*
>
> Detective Sergeant Symonds talking to 'Michael Smith'. Part of a taped conversation between a London detective and a London crook, which began the Times inquiry.

When, after March 1st, threats and harassment began, those involved in the public Inquiry, the defence group and the investigation were faced with two seemingly divergent theoretical propositions, each assuming that a different agency was responsible. The first assumed that because it was the Home Secretary who had visited the University and as this involved numbers of Special Branch officers, this agency would have 'dropped markers' on various activists involved in the demonstration and its organisation. Officers from this agency would then have become involved in threats and attacks.

The second proposition assumed something quite different; that the attacks and the harassment grew directly from the battle on the steps and the ensuing complaints, and that the harassment was *one* facet of an organised campaign mounted by low ranking officers and constables who found themselves suddenly open to public scrutiny and criticism. This proposition assumed that the organisation of the harassment involved some twenty to thirty officers, both plain clothes and uniformed, while doing their normal divisional duties.

The thesis of this book follows the second proposition, to which everything the investigation and the campaign later threw up, drew those working on the case, like a magnet. It is also apparent that the first proposition does not at the end of the day stand up to logical or rational scrutiny.

The first and most compelling argument against it is that of organisation. If we believe that the Special Branch targetted a handful of student activists, and that these individuals were harassed by, amongst others, uniformed officers, then we have to assume a mode of organisation; a chain of communication.[48] Of course, it could all have been done with a nod and a wink, even through impersonal information scattered on the police computer. Files on these individuals, open through VDU's in police stations, could have displayed commands to stop, search and harass. However, this kind of uncoordinated and impersonally organised conspiracy would have left much to chance.

The second argument which militates against the harassment *being organised* by the Special Branch, or another such agency, is the matter of motive. The Special Branch is a well established institution and it is also a well organised one. Like all agencies of the State it has a *modus operandi* which serves the political purpose of its masters. These goals are simply spelt out; to protect the State from subversion and with this in mind, to collect and collate intelligence on those people who might wish to overthrow the State by force or by organised propanganda. If this is a fair assessment, then it would be reasonable to assume that Special Branch officers are unlikely to become involved in overt operations of violent threat and attack against isolated students. Such operations in terms of priorities would be counter productive, not only would they drive activists to ground, but they would increase the chances of sudden and embarassing exposure.

We must also assume a certain level of intelligence and sophistication on the part of the Special Branch. Everything which we know about them tells us that for covert operations involving violence or break-ins and such things as 'counter-gang' bombings and even deep penetration, they will employ individuals from outside their own agency; private detectives, professional criminals or informers.

These arguments are not complete and they do not allow for some dual form of organisation in which the Special Branch provides intelligence and then, through informal mechanisms 'allows' uniformed or plain clothes officers to act out their policy on the ground. We have, as well, to guard against envisaging the Special Branch as a monolithic organisation which carries out its work in complete separation from the other police officers in the force. Over the last few years, constabulary forces, which all have Special Branch contingents, have adopted a policy of 'placing' Special Branch officers in very ordinary policing jobs, such as community liaison and even the Juvenile Bureau. The Special Branch contingent of any constabulary will work with force policy, and apart from the interests of national State security, will be involved in those areas which their Chief Constable directs them to be involved in. We know that in Manchester, the Operational Support Group (crime) draws together officers working in different squads. Whether or not there was some higher authority for the harassment of certain students after March 1st, it is likely that the plain clothes contingent of any operation would include officers from different squads, particularly those whose work would involve an intimate knowledge of the student population (Drugs Squad) and those who spent long periods on surveillance duties, Burglary and Stolen Car Squads, for example, and probably Special Branch officers.

In trying to resolve the question of the organisation and identity of those officers who harassed Steve Shaw and Sarah Hollis, we have to keep our minds open to the possibility of both a higher authority and the involvement of Special Branch officers. However, the thesis of this book follows the second hypothesis, that of an organised campaign mounted by low ranking officers who found themselves open to public scrutiny, for one main reason. In the investigation of crime, if we lack proof of a motive, we have to assume one. There has to be a cause, a primary mechanism. Without this, we would be working in a world which made no sense.

We live within a capitalist society with a highly developed State. The State deals with its opposition *at this time* in England, in a variety of ways, the majority of which are legislative, legalised or culturally well integrated within the social system. If this were not the case, every activist, every dissenter, would be open to random harassment and abuse. If the system were in terminal crisis, perhaps this would be the case, everyone on the left would suffer attacks, harassment and exposure from forces working for the State. This condition has not yet been reached in England.

The causal relationship between Sarah Hollis, Steven Shaw and the harassment which followed them for a year was, without doubt, the visit of Leon Brittan to Manchester University Student's Union, and the catalyst which brought the police and these students into conflict was the police operation to clear the steps together with the ensuing complaints.

The violent police operation that evening was both a crime in itself and the cause of further crimes. That evening provided the very personal and subjective motivation for a relatively large number of constables and lower ranking officers to conduct a covert campaign against a number of students and others who might, by accident or design, expose their original violence.

We have no way of knowing whether an organisational base already existed to protect these officers. The fact that Steven Shaw's flat was burgled and papers stolen within four days of the demonstration leads us to suspect that an organisation of some complexity already existed. This type of organisation which exists within, but is independent of, the structural hierarchy of the broader police force, has been recognised for some time as a 'firm within a firm.' An organisation which has different goals and objectives from that of its parent body, but which the parent body 'allows' to grow because some of its broader objectives overlap. Previous research into this area of police behaviour has focussed upon graft and financial corruption.[49] The 'firm within a firm' described in this book has grown out of another form of corruption involving career power and the illegal use of physical violence.

Large internal investigations into multiple complaints against the police are exceptionally prone to interference from the officers under investigation. They are therefore liable to uncover, or at least come into conflict with, already established firms within the firm. Despite the creation of the new 'independent' Police Complaints Authority, recent research shows that some 50% of complaints against the police are withdrawn, many because of fear of reprisals by the original offender.[50]

After the Times newspaper had exposed a firm within a firm inside the Metropolitan police in 1969, Frank Williamson, then an Her Majesty's Inspector of Constabularies, was called in to investigate the allegations. He was met on his arrival in London with a veritable defensive wall of obstruction which developed into telephone tapping and mail intercepts and attempts to intimidate his staff. The senior officer whom he had brought with him suffered severe nervous exhaustion and had to be taken off the case. After his departure Williamson was saddled with officers drawn from the Met. who were themselves already involved in corruption and active within the firm within a firm.[51]

In 1979, Operation Countryman was set up to investigate

allegations of criminal activities by officers within the City of London police force. Within weeks of their arrival in London from Avon and Somerset their headquarters were burgled and important papers stolen. From an original list of over eighty suspected officers, they managed, at the end of their inquiry, to gain a conviction against only one. Their inquiries were dogged by obstruction, witnesses were bribed and one disappeared.[52] They were continually under surveillance; they were harassed and their families threatened.[53] Ironically, the latest example of obstruction of an internal investigation has involved the Deputy Chief Constable of the Greater Manchester police, John Stalker.

However, this war between different constabularies is probably becoming a thing of the past. Since the late seventies much has been done to consolidate the position of a national police force, which works much more as a total institution. The concept of a national force has repercussions not only at the summit of its organisation, but also for the smaller firms within the firm inside the major cities. If there is a new co-ordination between constabularies at a national level, there is also a new spirit of co-operation between the aspiring but corrupt firms within the parent company.

The firm within a firm is a complex organisation, a corrupt conspiracy which has access to all the technology, the facilities and much of the personnel within certain ranks of the host organisation. It is a cancer which saps the strength of the host and finally usurps the power and the functions, in a deformed way, of the original institution. Its driving motivations are two fold; it defends and protects both the careers and the criminality of the officers who are committed to it, while at the same time perpetuating and developing its own organisation, out to gain control of further areas of corrupt practices.

In the beginning the firm survives because senior officers turn a blind eye to its cultural and political precepts, which appear at that time, to be only slight exaggerations of the dominant culture of the institution. As the firm grows and is seen by its members as being able to protect them, its precepts become more extreme. Ultimately senior officers are forced either to defend those involved or bury their heads in the sand and deny the firm's existence. Gradually the values of the firm within the firm become the prevailing values; at this point, those officers who find these values indefensible leave the force, vacating the ground to an ever growing parasite.

We cannot find, or even believe in this firm within a firm if we believe that economic or political corruption is guided directly by structural orders from the State itself. This would mean that the State specifically needed a majority of its officers to be involved in this kind of corrupt and undisciplined work. The State actually prefers to create loyalty in its police force by paying high wages and holding out the possibility of political power for ranking officers. It is only when it is at the point of collapse that the State resorts to the employment of criminal elements within the force. And although it might be the case that the corrupt firm within a firm serves the State, or 'does the State's job,' at the same time its autonomous organisation, makes it a danger to the coordinated power of the State.

The firm within a firm can become so powerful in its own right, especially when it works with professional criminals and illegitimate business interests that it can challenge the political and economic constitutional State. It was by virtue of this gradual process that Al Capone came to control the police force, the politicians and the business community of Chicago in the late 1920's.

The firm within a firm feeds not off direct orders from State agencies but by developing and accentuating aspects of the prevailing culture and ideology within its host institution. The firm within a firm is to the institution of the police service, and the rule of law, what the criminal economy is to the prevailing structure of business. If the prevailing economic climate is competetive, criminals are extremely competitive; if the prevailing culture is chauvinist, racist or sexist, then criminal culture tends to be more so, or at least more openly so. If the prevailing business culture believes in making a fast buck by cutting corners, the criminal world makes a faster buck and leaves no corners.

To find the firm within the firm, we look to the cultural and political values of the police force, not to their structure. We have to look for accentuations of ordinary police practices, to observe those officers who will go that little bit further than even the prevailing culture will condone. But the firm like all criminal organisations, is so powerful, so secretive and so adept, at using deceit and the mechanisms of power, that its structure is almost entirely hidden. It is a conspiracy which because of commonly held values, language and illegal money, or illegitimate power, needs only a nod and a wink to activate it.

Chapter Six

Fear on the Streets: March

In this way colleague protection becomes part of the unwritten police code. It is a code which 'covers up' for the deviant policeman, so much so that in some forces the 'honest cop' becomes the exception.

Tom Bowden: Beyond the Limits of the Law

Four days after the assault on the steps, forces were beginning to coalesce over the incident. For young people with little experience of work and the world outside the university, the core of student activists within the union organised with exemplary speed and intelligence to defend themselves and their friends who had been beaten or arrested.

By the afternoon of Monday March 4th, the students had gathered together statements from a large number of those present on the night. A delegate group had met once with the Manchester City Council Monitoring Unit and they had collected 500 signatures from union members calling for an extraordinary general meeting of the student body on the following afternoon.

The press, with the exception of the *Daily Mail*, was generally sympathetic to the demonstrators[54], and even the *Manchester Evening News*, not renowned for its championing of civil rights, was stating the case for them clearly against the police attack.

Manchester City Council was by this time priming the mechanisms which they would have to use in order to carry out some form of public inquiry. Although the politicians were at pains to work through proper constitutional channels, first approaching the Greater Manchester Police Authority for an inquiry, they did not deviate or procrastinate in their principal objective; to hold a public and independent inquiry.

The one voice at this time which echoed and thereby supported the silence of the Greater Manchester Police on the matter, was that of the University administration. This was the silence of a careful bureaucracy, not necessarily the silence of reaction. In private, individuals within the university hierarchy were voicing muted but opposing views. On the one hand were those who defended their backs with off hand remarks about the student demonstration having been attended by outsiders. This scapegoating gave them a certain relief from the responsibility which they should have shouldered on behalf of the students. Others made it clear that they thought the continuing visits by government ministers to the universities were acts of planned provocation. The official silence of the University authorities, however, continued to be a seminal weakness in the campaign which began to enlist support for a public and independent inquiry.

On Tuesday March 5th, at 5.00pm, seven hours or so after Steven Shaw had discovered his thesis material stolen, about twelve hundred students gathered in Whitworth Hall to debate a vote of no confidence in four members of the Students Union executive. The motion was proposed by those who had organised the demonstration and were now organising the defence campaign and the call for an inquiry.

The five part motion was couched in uncompromising terms. It expressed outrage at the police behaviour on the night; no confidence in any police investigation; the demand for a public inquiry; a complete moratorium on co-operation between the students union and the GMP and no confidence in four members of the executive.

By this time, what had occurred within the building on the night was known to some of the students. But because the union executive had negotiated with the police from an apparent position of trust, and because everything which happened on the night showed that in comparison to the police, they were disorganised and had been hopelessly misled, none of the union executive felt prepared to take individual responsibility.

A short time before the police had charged the students, the Union General Secretary had ordered the Union security staff to lock the main front doors. One of the central questions to be answered at the meeting became, in whose interest was it to lock the doors? When Michael Heseltine had visited the University the year before, students had taken control of the corridors and stairways of their building and TAG officers had stormed up the stairs creating a way out for him. On March 1st. the police must have been determined to control the inside of the building as well as its entrance. Had the executive of the union, made the decision to lock the doors with the police? Was this the right decision?

The meeting in Whitworth Hall lasted five hours; by its conclusion the number of participants had fallen to six hundred. After a number of votes on amendments, the vote of no confidence got through as a motion of censure. The motion on non-cooperation with the police was passed in a watered down version which called upon the executive to draw up guidelines and protocol. But the part of the motion which referred to non-co-operation with any police complaints inquiry was passed, against the wishes of the executive, and became union policy.

It was this meeting which began laying the ground for a slowly developing isolation of the radicals. The meeting split the union between those who were willing to work within the framework of a police controlled investigation, and those who continued to demand a thoroughly independent and public inquiry. From this time onwards, while some members and officers of the executive were to throw in their lot personally with what would be the Avon and Somerset inquiry, a large part of the student body refused to have anything to do with it.

Although there was no democratic discussion organised for the academic staff at the university on the issue, the administration also placed itself in support of the internal police inquiry. Steven Shaw was one of the students at the meeting who knew in principle that he did not want an inquiry conducted by the police. He had not reported the break in at his flat to the police and he was already beginning to suspect their involvement. Steve went to stay with friends and did not return to Top of the Meadow Farm except during the day time to pick up papers.

He had no better explanation of what had happened than did his friends but he thought that there must be a connection between his meeting at the council monitoring unit, his custody of the statements, and the break-in. Although not anticipating any further problems and certainly not anticipating the return of his thesis material, he decided to 'lay low' for a while.

On Wednesday March 6th, at 9.15am, Steve left a friend's house to drive to the University. Driving along the Stockport Road, a main arterial road running into Manchester centre, he passed within half a mile of Longsight police station where officers had been briefed on the night of March 1st. It was the tail end of the rush hour. On Stockport Road, near the traffic lights, he noticed a white police car driving slowly behind him. The car flashed its lights and Steve stopped.

The police car stopped behind him. A police officer left the passenger side of the car, walked over to Steve and accused him of speeding. Following a short argument, the officer who had first asked him to produce his documents, requested him to follow the police car to Levenshulme police station. Steve parked his car outside the station and went in with the police passenger. The policeman approached the desk sergeant and began a discussion about Steve's case of speeding. The desk sergeant, an overweight man in his late forties, asked Steve for his name and address, then asked him why he had refused to accept an HO/RTI.[55] Steve explained that he had not been speeding. The conversation was convivial, and not at all threatening; until suddenly the sergeant paused for a moment:

> He looked down at the name and address and then said, "You're the chap making allegations about your thesis aren't you?"

The voice was casual and unconcerned but Steve was thrown into panic. Only a few close friends knew about the burglary. He answered the question in a non-committal manner, accepted an HO/RTI from the officer and left the station.

It was only six days after the Brittan visit but Steve was becoming conscious of being pulled down into something which was beyond his comprehension or his control. At that time, it was only an anxiety, a vague and grey worry. The rest of the week passed uneventfully, Steve worked with others on a leaflet for the first court cases which were due to come up the following week. He presented his documents at Levenshulme police station; they were taken away, brought back, and he left. Nothing untoward was said to him. All the things which had happened so far, could be thought about later and might have been imagined; it was easy to mishear someone.

The first remand hearing for the students arrested on March 1st, were due to be held on Friday March 15th, at Manchester magistrates court. Frequent defence meetings with three solicitors had resolved a strategy for this hearing. Through the solicitors, the thirty three students were going to plead 'collective self defence.' A picket had been organised outside the court and buses laid on from the University. On the morning, two hundred students turned out for the picket; Steven Shaw, however, was late arriving and rough words were spoken by his closest friends about his time keeping.

The night before the hearing, Steve had stayed with friends in West Didsbury. He set off around nine in the morning to ensure that he got to court in plenty of time. Almost at the end of Palatine Road, a white Metro police car pulled into the traffic behind him and flashed him down. This time, both uniformed officers decamped from the car and walked over; one spoke to Steve through the driver's window while the other made a cursory inspection of his car. The officer accused him of speeding and commented on the safety of one of his back tyres. Again the conversation was perfunctory, Steve accepted an HO/RTI and was allowed to proceed. Later that day, he produced his documents at Longsight police station.

The beginning of the student's cases coincided roughly with the end of the Jackie Berkeley trial and parallels were already being drawn by black and white activists between her case and what was now happening to Steve Shaw. At the end of March, Steve returned to his family in London where he began to re-assemble the material for his thesis and making contact with a number of London researchers whose help he had sought previously.

Chapter Seven

Fear on the Streets: April

This small fiction that are honest and would report illegal activity are ostracised. Nobody will work with them. They look at them like they're a freak, and they are a freak.

E.R. Stoddard: The Informal Code of Police Deviancy: A Group Approach to Blue Coat Crime. (Quoted in Tom Bowden: Beyond the Limits of the Law).

Throughout April, while Steve was working in London, two different groups were organising inquiries into what had happened on March 1st. James Anderton in consultation with John Stalker his deputy had by now made a decision to call in an outside force to handle the many complaints against his officers. Although representatives of both camps would have claimed that it was their intention to get to the 'truth', there were seminal and oppositional differences in the way that they were going about it. Furthermore, the resources of the groups were unequal. While the Greater Manchester Police had all the information at their disposal and the ability to call in other police officers supposedly used to carrying out investigations[56], Manchester City Council had only their committment to truth and very limited financial resources. Apart from the stories of the people they represented, they were working in the dark.

The first move by Manchester City Council was to call upon the GMP Authority to demand an inquiry under section 32 of the 1964 Police Act.[57] This request was made both to the Chief Constable and the Home Secretary; as expected it was turned down. They then did want they had known from the start they would have to do; set up their own inquiry. By the middle of April, the committee processes had agreed the funding and the organisation of such an inquiry. By the end of April, discussions between the Police Monitoring Unit, the Police Monitoring Committee and senior council officers had formulated a list of prospective panellists for the inquiry team.

Meanwhile, at Chester House, the headquarters of Greater Manchester Police, James Anderton was reportedly beginning to show irritation.[58] As far as the GMP were concerned there was little to substantiate the need for an enquiry. By the end of the week following

Brittan's visit, however, a number of students not closely involved with the political centre of the union had taken their own initiative and made individual complaints against GMP officers. These students received letters from the Deputy Chief Constable, John Stalker, informing them that they would be visited by senior officers who handled complaints within the GMP.[59]

By March 8th, one of the complainants had received a visit from two Inspectors attached to 'Y' Dept, the complaints investigation department of the GMP. They asked the complainant if he had acted alone or in concert with others and then explained to him the process for making a formal complaint. They gave him the Home Office publication 'Police and Public: Complaints against the police — Police Acts 1964 and 1976.' They also told him that they had no doubt an inquiry would be set up into what had happened on March 1st, and that in all probability this inquiry would cover his complaint.

Before the officers left they asked the complainant how Sarah Hollis was and whether he had seen her fall down the steps. Fortunately for the complainant, he had not seen this incident. The officers left asking the student to consider whether he wished to make a formal complaint or whether he would he happy for his complaint to come under the general auspices of a police inquiry.

The officers returned that afternoon, when the complainant signed a statement to the effect that he did not wish to make a formal complaint as he was now assured that there would be an inquiry. On this occassion, the police asked whether the student had spoken to anyone about his complaint. When he said he had, they noted this information and left. Another student who made a similar formal complaint was asked whether he had any leaflets or documents which might help the police inquiry.

On March 11th, Deputy Chief Constable John Reddington, who was to head the Avon and Somerset inquiry in its initial stages, arrived in Manchester. By the end of April both inquiries were in their initial stages, Manchester City Council's determination to pursue an inquiry, together with discussions which must have taken place between the Chief Constable and the Home Office, had forced Anderton's hand and the whole matter was handed over to the new Police Complaints Authority which came into being on April 29th. From May, the PCA took complete control of the investigation. It would be their task normally to choose and oversee a team of officers, but in this case, they stayed with the ones that the GMP had chosen.

We can only guess at the feelings and thoughts of those officers who had been involved in policing the demonstration on March 1st. In response to growing government initiatives on public order, with the government wanting to push through some kind of Bill on 'freedom of speech' and working within a constabulary where the Chief Constable had always encouraged a hard line, they had been instructed to police the steps in a certain way. They had done an efficient job using all their attributes of training and culture; now, all around them, disquiet was being expressed. Not only was there to be an independent and public inquiry run by the Labour controlled city council, but there was also to be an inquiry asked for by their own Chief Constable, involving officers from another force.

As if all this was not enough, the court hearing of the arrested students began at the beginning of April and would run continuously for the next two months. The court cases were the most vulnerable point of public exposure with regard to police tactics generally and the violence of individual officers in particular. With 'clever left wing lawyers' and 'undependable Magistrates,' together with a crumbling fabric of public order law, who knew what might happen.

The public galleries of courts in which the students appeared were packed by the campaign during every trial. A small but persistent picket symbolically 'held' another set of steps, those leading to the court complex.

With Steven Shaw away in London, officers of the GMP began surveillance on other student activists who had been associated with him and the demonstration. One archaeology student in particular, who had been active in the Berkeley campaign and in the new defence campaign, found his life suddenly disrupted. Steve had stayed with Dom Wall following the burglary of his flat. Dom lived with a group of people who had been politically active at the University.

On Tuesday April 23rd, a woman living in the house noticed a police van parked across the road. A sergeant stood by the van, talking into his radio whenever he observed movements at the window. The students in the house, fearing that they were going to be raided, hid or destroyed any information they had about the Leon Brittan visit, and then left the house for the protection of the students union. Two hours later, on their return to the house, the police van had left. But as they walked into the wide, tree lined road, they saw that it had been replaced by an orange Avenger, again parked directly opposite their house. The occupants were two men in their mid twenties wearing casual clothes.

Instead of going into the house, they went to a cafe and discussed their situation. It was decided that Dom would stay with friends while the others went back to the house to get the books he needed for his exam revision. When the group came back out of their house, the Avenger had moved but one of the occupants was standing about thirty yards down the road drinking a can of Coke. Dom was given the books and he left for a safer house. When his friends returned to the house a second time, a new Marina car was parked there; the man who had been drinking Coke was now a passenger in this car, which stayed outside the house until 10.00pm. Its registration number was taken and it has since been found to belong to the Greater Manchester Police.

The heat was on. But no one who felt its warmth could have any conception of the origins or the size of the phenomenon; neither could they know whether they were pitted against a few rogue officers who wanted simply to intimidate witnesses, or an organised campaign of harassment. The picture of a conspiracy comes into focus slowly and can only be seen by someone who has a complete overview, or by the whole collective body which is its victim.

Throughout April, Steven Shaw did his best to keep in touch with friends and to help others taking their exams with information. During this period, he sent essays on Latin American politics to a woman in Dom Wall's house, who was taking the same degree; they never arrived. Neither did personal letters sent to a close woman friend during the same period.

On Monday April 29th, Charles Alcock, who had been attacked by officers at the top of the union steps, came up for trial in the Magistrates Court. Sarah Hollis was one of his witnesses. She had seen him attacked and had stepped towards him and shouted, before being flung down the steps and knocked unconscious. Sarah Hollis was a good witness for Charles Alcock. She came from an impeccable middle class background, she was young, bright and committed to humanitarian views. Even the police at their most prejudiced could not accuse her of being the kind of person who was wasting tax payers money. Besides this, she had not originally been part of the demonstration on the steps.

On April 29th, Sarah appeared in court on Alcock's behalf, still wearing the neck collar made necessary by her injuries. Alcock's solicitor, in taking her through her evidence, made the point that she would be making a complaint against the police. The Magistrate aquitted Alcock. The motive for the brief flurry of violence acted out by a small number of officers leaving the union was now thrown into question. If Alcock had been aquitted mainly on Sarah Hollis's evidence, then her own complaint, even without the name or number of the officer who had thrown her down the steps, was more of an open and shut case. The nightmare for Sarah Hollis was just about to begin.

As Sarah cycled home from the Magistrates Court, a distinctive white van belonging to the GMP crawled behind her; it went slowly enough to intimidate her and continued with her long enough for her to understand that she was now a target.

Chapter Eight

Fear on the Streets: May

The evidence is that the police loyalty and solidarity is often sufficiently strong to make them tolerant of their own crime; that is of police action beyond the limits of the law.

Tom Bowden: Beyond the Limits of the Law

The Police Complaints Authority took over administrative responsibility for the Avon and Somerset officers already chosen by James Anderton and John Stalker to conduct the investigation into the events of March 1st. The investigation was to be a test of the new Police Complaints Authority, which was set up under the 1984 Police and Criminal Evidence Act. It was the first major inquiry by an outside force to fall within the Authority's jurisdiction.

The Police Complaints Authority consists of twelve members including a chairman and two deputy chairmen. From its inception doubts were raised about its ability to act independently. But it was not simply its independence, its ability to act autonomously, which was in question. Anyone who has investigated corrupt police officers understands that they are very plausible and more than capable of reassuring senior officers and outside observers. How would the Complaints Authority sitting in the aministrative comfort of its London offices know whether the police investigators were doing their job properly? How would they know whether a report·submitted to them was an accurate picture of what happened or a straightforward cover-up? If middle management officers involved in corruption and brutality were able to convince even Chief Constables that critcisms were without foundation, how much more easily could investigating officers hoodwink an isolated group of civilians in London?

Suggestions that the new Complaints Authority could be independent, or could act with an incisive commitment in cases which were politically important, was viewed with suspicion by the majority of students and many of the Manchester City Council officers who were now working on the cases. Their fears appeared to be justified when it was found that officers from Avon and Somerset were billeted at

Sedgley Park, the Greater Manchester Police training centre, where they were thrown cheek to jowl into contact with senior Manchester officers. Officers from the two forces drank and socialised together but led those they interviewed to believe that they never discussed the case.

Disquiet was increased by the early reports which began to circulate on their methods of investigation. Some students began to wonder exactly who it was who had been accused of committing offences.[60] While GMP officers involved in the disturbance were sent questionnaires, students were tracked down and subject to long interviews at all times of the day and night. Students' home addresses and telephone numbers were acquired and their parents rung to obtain their Manchester addresses. It is true that the police were working within an uncooperative environment as far as the students were concerned, but their early and obvious attitudes to the case did nothing to persuade people that they would be either sympathetic or independent.

Avon and Somerset officers began trying to elicit the names of students who had been present on March 1st, in a more or less random fashion. They already had the names and addresses of those who had been arrested, and they gleaned others from a variety of sources, most particularly vulnerable students, some of whom gave the names of as many as twenty other demonstrators. While their early enquiries within the student body met with minimal success, they were given greater help by officers of the union executive and more particularly the Vice Chancellor of the University. After a few weeks of their investigation, the University authorities provided them with an office in the Anglican Chaplaincy and aided them in the posting of notices throughout the university asking witnesses and complainants to come forward.

Sadly, this sort of naive and face saving co-operation by official bodies with the police, against the wishes of those for whom they assume a responsibility and without any understanding of police behaviour, can lead to jeopardy and danger for those involved. By colluding with the Avon and Somerset Inquiry the University administration was giving official sanction to something which would cut off any escape route for the students who were being harassed and threatened.

In order to repair the damage which they had already done by not coming out in support of the students after the events of March 1st., the University authorities should have backed the students in support of the Manchester City Council Inquiry. Even if they did not wish to do this, they could at least have made available legal advice for students rather than simply surrendering them to the police. Their continuing faith in the police reinforced a cycle of liberal degeneracy from which they were later unable to extricate themselves. This attitude contrasted sharply with that of the academic staff and their union the AUT. From the beginning the AUT had wanted to make the police attack on the students an issue, linking it to other forms of State intervention in the universities[61].

By the end of May all pretentions to independence with respect to the Avon and Somerset inquiry went up in smoke when it was learnt that statements taken from witnesses by Avon and Somerset Officers had been handed to the GMP prosecuting solicitors but not to defence solicitor for use in the cases against arrested students. This had apparently been done on instructions from the Director of Public Prosecutions. The Complaints Authority rather than defend its autonomy in this crucial matter had simply acquiesced. Defence solicitors met with the PCA and John Reddington, the head of the investigation, to protest.

During May, while Avon and Somerset officers were openly scouring Manchester for information, and while the court cases were continuing, Greater Manchester Police officers were stepping up their campaign of intimidation and harassment.

On May 9th. Dom Wall was walking home along Wilmslow Road, not far from his house, when a red Ford Cortina suddenly pulled out from the flow of traffic and shadowed him, driving slowly along the curb as he walked. He saw both the occupants with reasonable clarity. They were in their thirties, wearing suits and ties; and both had dark hair and one had a moustache. The car continued alongside of him at walking pace for about fifteen yards; neither of the men said anything. It then accelerated and continued slowly in front of him for a further two hundred yards or so. At this time, the significance of the red Ford Cortina which had been parked near the students union building on March 1st, and which it was later discovered was a police car, had not emerged.

On the same day, Steve Shaw, who had arrived back in Manchester and was staying with friends, was stopped for a third time on a traffic violation. He was returning alone from the University at about 5.30pm. Driving along Wilmslow Road, in the centre of Rusholme, a police Rover car drew in behind him and flashed its lights. The officer who approached the car, accused Steven of speeding and claimed that one of his rear tyres was bald. He was again given an HO/RTI and told to produce his documents.

At 3.00am, on Monday 10th, Sarah Hollis received the first of what was to become a series of strange anonymous phone calls. When she picked up the receiver the line went dead. By now, the strands of a conspiracy were beginning to weave themselves together in the minds of the victims. Everything that happened was discussed either in the students' union or with council officers in the Police Monitoring Unit. Although no one had anything resembling an answer as to why it was happening, what the students were up against was slowly dragging itself from the deep and beginning to lumber into view.

Later on May 10th, Steve attended one of a number of Student Union executive meetings held during this period to re-discuss cooperation with the Avon and Somerset inquiry. Some of the executive officers felt unnecessarily constrained by the vote of the student body and were determined to give the support of the union to the police[62]. Steve spoke against this proposition. Late that night, Sarah Hollis, alone in her flat in John Nash Crescent, received another anonymous phone call.

On Saturday May 11th, with Steven Shaw at home again in London, Sarah was cycling through Manchester in the afternoon. Manchester City F.C. had a home game and the streets were full of fans wandering in a slow stream towards the Main Road ground. Suddenly Sarah was stopped by two uniformed motorcycle policemen, questioned about where she was going and asked to give her name and address.

Undoubtedly, the police already had Sarah's address and the purpose of her being stopped could only have been harassment. By now, to anyone who might have been watching from an objective distance, the beast lumbering from the deep was assuming the most sinister proportions. Just how great was the intelligence and what was the scope of the instructions received by officers of the GMP to target these students?

★ ★ ★

Sarah Hollis lived, at that time, in John Nash Crescent, Hulme. It was an estate build as part of a slum clearance project in the late sixties. Little loved by anyone who lives there, it is nevertheless inhabited by many students because of the concessionary rents. Sociologists and architects could no doubt debate to eternity whether this new slum is worse than the one it replaced, but at least the old terraces, crammed and grimy, were evenly inhabited. The residents of John Nash crescent have voted against the architectural award given its designers with their feet, and occasionally with arson.

Dogs are now the only creatures which feel at home in the crescents. Property after property has been abandoned, the work of fire and vandalism are the predominant architectural motifs. Ground level garages are unused and unsecured, the grass arena around which the flats are built is overgrown and littered with glass, bricks and dog shit. Residents brave enough to face the damp and destruction, or poor enough to have no choice, can expect to be robbed and burgled with a constancy which makes front doors virtually pointless.

In May 1985, in addition to Sarah Hollis, the residents of John Nash Crescent included a young woman named Amanda Hughes and many doors along on another level, a young man named Frank Logan. Both of these young people had been in trouble with the police and both had been under the protection and guidance of probation officers. Frank Logan, when he was not occupied in doing up cars and trying to sell them, had stolen or 'rung' them. He was an isolated lad, who had no real ambitions within Manchester's criminal world; in the main, he just got by. He knew a few of the thieves and criminal families scattered across Manchester, but his last period in remand home had shaken his confidence about working his way into the fraternity.

Amanda Hughes was an energetic and excitable young woman, far more astute than the first impression she might give. Her thoughts shift with speed behind her eyes, considering all the angles before she answers with apparent nervous spontaneity. She had convictions for burglary. But she too, was beginning to pull herself out of her poor start, making a home for herself, her baby and a good relationship with a male friend.

In May 1985, Amanda and Frank were casually acquainted through being in and around the area of John Nash Crescent. They had never done criminal work together, and while Frank kept very much to himself with respect to the cars he worked on, Amanda, who was more involved in burglary, tended to work with close male friends. Her common law husband was in prison at this time and she had just managed to get her small child out of care. Amanda's child and her bloke were really the only things she had going for her. In May she was on police bail, having been found on the premises of a house in Chorlton.

These two young people had different attitudes to the police. Amanda's frequent involvement with them, when she had broken the law; her involvement with some male officers through her work; and her identification with a number of female detectives, had created a kind of bond between her and the police officers in the area. Frank's relationship with the police was perhaps more traditionally male. He thought of them as good and bad by degree but preferred not to get too close to them; unless of course he needed a favour.

In the early hours of Monday May 13th, Amanda Hughes and Frank Logan burgled the flat of Sarah Hollis. In an amateur, arduous and completely disorganised burglary which lasted hours and with Sarah Hollis deeply asleep on her bed, Amanda, who had entered through a front window, passed out to Frank a number of electrical appliances and various other of Sara's personal possessions. This burglary was one of five which can be located at the centre of the conspiracy against the Manchester students. It was however, the only one to be solved, and even then, its solving left more questions than answers.

Frank Logan is forthcoming, if apparently confused, about how and why he became involved in the burglary. He says that two weeks before, he was approached in the John Nash shopping precinct near the Crescent by two detectives whom he knew by name from previous offences. In the course of a completely informal conversation with these officers, it was, he says, put to him that if he had nothing better to do and if he was contemplating any criminal activity, he might break into Sarah Hollis's flat. He was told what the flat looked like from the outside and about a distinctive poster which was in the window.[63]

Burglary was not Frank's forte however, and he put the conversation down to police pathology; a pathology which was way beyond his comprehension as a small time crook. Some days after this incident, Frank says that Amanda came to him asking if he fancied doing a burglary with her. He didn't demur from this and he says that he went through the local phone directory *with* Amanda looking for telephone numbers in John Nash Crescent. Finally, between them, they came up with a number which, when called, received no answer. The two of them went to burgle the flat which belonged to that phone number. When they arrived at the premises, and on seeing the poster in the window, Frank realised that the flat belonged to Sarah Hollis.

While Frank stood outside, Amanda went into the flat. She came out almost immediately and told him that Sarah Hollis was asleep on her bed. Frank was in favour of dropping the project completely but Amanda, who was very excited, insisted upon going ahead.

Following the burglary, they sat in Amanda's flat dividing up the proceeds. Frank Logan has all along been adamant that he never saw any papers or documents amongst the stolen items. By the following morning, when Sarah made a full inventory of what was missing to a constable who visited her at home, two witness statements which formed the basis of her complaint against the police were missing from her flat. The only other fact which made the burglary peculiar was that someone had left an open stanley knife next to Sarah's bed.

Six weeks after the burglary occurred, police officers from Greenheys Lane police station, literally round the corner, called at Amanda's address in the early hours of the morning and took her into custody. A few hours later, Frank Logan was also arrested. While in custody, Frank said next to nothing, but he was then presented with a statement which Amanda had made, and which implicated them both in the burglary. As a consequence of this, Frank also made a statement and they both admitted the offence. While in custody, in the early hours of the morning, Frank Logan was visited by officers from the Avon and Somerset inquiry. He did not tell them about the police involvement and, surprisingly, he was not asked one question about any statements or any untoward motive for chosing to burgle that flat in particular. Sarah Hollis was later told by one of the Avon and Somerset officers, while he was attempting to gain her trust, that he had been instrumental in getting her burglary solved.

At trial, Frank Logan was sent to prison for six months and Amanda Hughes had her probation order extended. Before we pass on from this episode, it is worth raising a number of questions. If police officers from Greenheys Lane made an approach to Frank Logan, who else in the same area had they approached? Had they approached Frank because another person, a burglar, had suggested to them them that Frank might be the person to help on a burglary? Was it simply coincidence that one of the officers whom Frank says approached him, a woman police detective, knew Amanda Hughes very well and had spoken with her on other occasions about Sarah Hollis?[64] If the witness statements went missing during the burglary, why did Frank not see them and why did Amanda deny having taken them? If the witness statements did not go missing during the burglary, when were they taken, and by whom? Were the previous anonymous phone calls which Sarah answered related to the burglary?

The police claimed in court that they had solved the crime after finding one of Amanda's finger prints on the window pane. Amanda however, had been arrested only two weeks before the burglary at Sarah's for a burglary in Chorlton. Why did it take six weeks to trace a finger print? Both Amanda and Frank are united in the view that they wiped the window clean on leaving. How did it happen that Amanda Hughes, with a record of previous offences, and having admitted that she was the person who actually effected the burglary, was given a lighter sentence than Frank Logan? Finally, how was it possible for an officer from the Avon and Somerset Constabulary, who was not meant to be in communication with GMP officers, to resolve a petty crime in John Nash Crescent which was apparently baffling the officers at the local police station who knew the burglars?

Of the two statements which were stolen from Sarah Hollis's flat, only one shed any light upon the attack at the top of the steps. This statement was made by Jeannette Entwistle and it had her home address at the top. A few weeks later, her house was burgled. Although all the rooms had been entered, with the exception of her own, they had been left in an orderly state. When she and her house mates returned from a short holiday, she found her room was strewn with papers and personal documents. And Jeannette said, "Who's been searching my room?" but neither Goldilocks or any of the little piglets were to be found.

The war against Sarah Hollis was coming closer. On Wednesday May 15th, two days after her flat had been burgled, Sarah, who had decided to give evidence to the Avon and Somerset inquiry, went with her solicitor to meet Assistant Chief Constable Reddington. After she had given a statement to another Avon and Somerset officer, Reddington suggested that she might have other matters to talk about. Sarah mentioned both her recent harassment and the burglary. Reddington then began shouting at her, demanding to know whether she was suggesting that police officers had been involved in these incidents. Sarah broke down in tears and left the room.

That same evening, as she was cycling home from the union building, a car pulled up behind her at a set of traffic lights and two men got out and approached her. They spoke only one short and threatening sentence.

> "Just remember, we can pick you up at any time we like, and we know the date of your exams."

Sarah was left shaken and frightened. Her week of hateful experiences was beginning to add up to a nightmare. What she did not know as she peddled away from the lights, was that the day before the screw had also tightened on Steven Shaw.

Five Hours in Bootle Street[65]

Steven Shaw had to work hard rewriting his thesis. With much of the original material missing the new version was neither so detailed nor so analytical. A part of the original thesis had been concerned with the riots which had occurred in Moss Side, Manchester and more generally in other inner city areas in 1981. The first set of material which Steven had gathered included documents which led him to believe that plain clothes officers had been acting as agents provocateur before the riots began. When his thesis material was stolen these documents went with it; they were seminal to his thesis, and he was unlikely to see them again.

On Saturday May 11th, Steve returned to London to collect the rewritten thesis, which his mother had been typing for him. The following Monday, having put it all together, he made a number of photocopies before catching the early afternoon train back to Manchester.

He was relieved at having finished the thesis, and pleased with the 60,000 word result. He was eager to hand it in to his tutor at the University. On Tuesday morning, he drove to the University and around lunch time handed the thesis to his professor's secretary. There was still one illustration which he needed from the police monitoring unit. He parked near Manchester Town Hall and walked across Albert Square. It was quiet and the massive gothic Town Hall, the square and its tall stone sculpture all reminded him of the civic pride that the large industrial cities must have had in the last century.

Then, as he approached the Town Hall entrance he noticed something which was out place. A heavy squat military blue TAG van sat facing the Town Hall, the mesh grill pushed back over its roof, its windows blackened. It was a sinister reminder that the work on his thesis was not an academic matter. Inside the police monitoring unit he picked up the picture of an ARWEN 37 baton round repeater gun[66]. He left the Town Hall, noticed that the TAG vehicle had now gone, and drove back to the University.

He reclaimed his thesis from the professor's secretary and inserted the illustration. When he shut it and gave it back he felt pleased at having done a good job. He walked out of the University with a weight off his mind and only his examinations now to worry about.

Driving back to Rusholme where he was going to stay with a woman friend, he felt a slight sense of loss, almost as if he had nothing to do now his thesis was finished. He stopped to fill the car with petrol and then remembered another small detail, something which he had forgotton to tell the professor's secretary.

He left the petrol station and drove slowly back towards the University, feeling relaxed. Suddenly, in his rear view mirror, he noticed a red car flashing its lights. It was about four thirty. He wasn't speeding, he didn't associate the car with the police; he continued driving. The red car pulled out from behind him and once past, turned sharply in, braking and boxing him. He braked suddenly and sat still.

In the few minutes before both doors of the car opened and two men strode towards him, he registered a few details of the car. At the time it didn't occur to him to drive off, or then to take its registration number. It was a bright afternoon, cars passed him and he could see children idling back from school. The car was a red W registration Ford Cortina, in good condition. The two men approached the passenger window of his car.

Steve wound down the window. The taller of the two men leant his hands on the window and pushed his face forwards. His voice was formal.

"Are you Steven David Shaw of Top of the Meadow Farm, Waterhead, Oldham?"

"Yes" Steve answered hesitantly.

The man took a small wallet from his jacket pocket and held it open at a plastic covered card. It was shut again before Steve had time to read it.

"We are police officers and we want to interview you. We are investigating the disturbances at the time of the Leon Brittan visit.''

Steve looked up. The officer had bad acne down the left side of his face. It was lined and strained and although his tone now was fairly pleasant, he didn't look as if he would brook any argument. The other officer was standing a couple of feet back. He was balding with a round face and looked slightly older than the man who had spoken. He was looking down imperiously, his hands in his pockets. Steve wanted to object but didn't know how to; he was only vaguely aware of his rights and anyway, they were never much use in a real situation.

''We'd like you to accompany us to Bootle Street police station.''

The officer was becoming impatient.

''Are you arresting me?'' It was all he could think of.

''No, you're not under arrest''.

''So I don't have to come with you?''

It was more of a plea than a question. The officer smiled slightly.

''No, you don't have to come with us, but if you don't come now, we can pull you in at three or four in the morning, keep you all night *and* get a warrant for your arrest. It's up to you.''

The officer leaned further forward. He was staring into Steve's eyes as if this made his point stronger.

''I think you had better come with us. We know where you live. We know where you're staying, we know your movements, you won't get shot of us easily.''

Steve had a sudden picture of being arrested at his friend's house early in the morning.

The officer stepped back from the car.

''Just follow us to Bootle Street.''

The two men walked back to their car and drove off slowly.

Following the car, his mind was full of confused thoughts. Momentarily, he took his eyes off the road and looked at the seat behind him. There were no copies of his thesis in the car; there was nothing in the car. Perhaps it would be a short interview; maybe they simply wanted evidence from him about the Brittan demonstration. The two cars drove up Oxford Road, past the University and into St. Peter's Square, in the heart of Manchester. Opposite the Free Trade Hall, the Cortina turned to the right and drove straight in under the stone arch of Bootle Street Police Station.[67] He followed and parked in the yard a few bays from their car. He wondered why he hadn't simply driven straight past, if it had been a film, he would have done; it was as if he had been hypnotised by the authority of the red car. Now his stomach was churning over and he felt sick. The two men walked over as he got out of the car and locked it.

''This way'', the shorter of the two beckoned with a wave of the hand.

The two men set off walking casually under the roofed garage area of the station to a door. Walking slowly behind them, he had a better chance to observe them. They were both very smart, one in a dark grey single breasted suit with narrow lapels, the other in a navy blue suit with a thin blue pin stripe. They both wore ties. The man with acne on his face, the younger of the two, was about six foot tall, while the other, the balding man, was about five foot eleven.[68] As the men opened the door and stepped into a corridor, Steve had a thought which was to re-occur again and again; were they too smart to be ordinary police officers? He wished that he had looked more closely at the warrant card; could they be Special Branch officers? The short corridor turned into another and he saw policemen in white shirts and heavy black uniforms moving about, carrying papers, going in and out of doors. At least here was the safety of other people.

One of the men opened a light coloured panelled door on the left of the corridor and the three of them entered a room.[69] Once inside Steve felt a surge of relief. This wasn't the cold stone of some anonymous cell block; perhaps after all it would be a civilised discussion. Most reassuring of all, it wasn't the kind of room that you got beaten up in.

The room, which was about ten foot by fifteen, was painted white. It had one window, quite high in the wall,[70] and fluorescent strip lighting on the ceiling. The lights were already on in the room. It was empty except for a black vinyl topped table with silver metal legs and three chairs, one on either side of the table and a third against the wall near the door. The chairs had metal legs and orange moulded plastic seats and backs. On the wall behind him he noticed an old fashioned round finned radiator. The floor was carpeted with a thin pile plain dark carpet. He walked over to the table in the middle of the room. For an institution like a police station the room had a certain dour taste. This was going to be a discussion and not an interrogation.

Steve sat down in the nearest chair, his back to the door. One of the officers stepped over to the wall and set down the third chair on the other side of the table with his companion. For a moment Steve leant forward on the table and then when that seemed too authoritative, he leant back and let his arms hang down by the sides of the chair.

The atmosphere in the room was tense, which made the silence more ominous. Suddenly the older of the two men, the balding one, got up, pushed the chair gently under the table and left the room. Steve heard the door close slowly behind him. Now, he thought he had chosen the wrong chair, he felt vulnerable, unable to see the door and what was happening behind him.

The man with the pock marked face looked at him across the table, one of his arms resting easily on it. There was no watch or jewellery on the hand which stretched flatly over the table top.

"What's your full name and date of birth?"

"Steven David Shaw, 23.8.62."

"And you live at Top of the Meadow Farm, Waterhead?"

"Yes"

The man had no note book or paper and nothing was being recorded. Steve decided as far as possible to stick to 'yes' or 'no' answers.

"Were you outside the union building on March 1st when the Home Secretary visited the University?"

"Yes"

"Did you help organise the demonstration?"

"No"

The man's tone was pleasant, almost disinterested; he spoke with an empty abstractedness as if he didn't care about the answers.

"Why did you go?"

"I don't know."

"Come on, did you agree with trying to stop Brittan speaking?"

"Not really, it was just a demonstration against the policies of the Conservative government."

The door opened behind him and the round faced man reappeared without his jacket.[71] While Steve continued to answer questions, out of the corner of his eye he saw the man in the background rolling up his sleeves. The man sat solidly on the remaining chair. Did this mean that he was about to get a thumping, his stomach sank. He glanced at the round faced man who stared back threateningly. Steve's eyes fell to his bare arms and he noticed a small white scar on the man's inside elbow.[72]

"Can I ring a solicitor?"

"No." The answer was quite definite.

"Will you make a note of the fact that I've asked for one?" Steve felt his voice shaking. The man with acne looked at his companion.

"It isn't necessary, you won't need a solicitor."

"Let's get something done." The round faced man looked serious, he leant forward resting his arms on the table.

"Why did you go to the Leon Brittan demonstration?"

"I don't know, because everyone else did I suppose."

He didn't want to make any definitive statements about his politics.

"You went because you violently disagree with the Conservative Government, didn't you?" The round faced man was very agressive.

"I wouldn't put it like that, but I don't agree with the way the miners' strike was policed and other things."

"Are you a socialist?"

"Yes"

"What kind of socialist are you?"

"Are you the sort that votes or the sort that believes in revolution?"

"I can't answer that question."

"Why not?" The man with acne had a gentler approach

"Because it's so stupid."

There was silence for a moment before the man with acne began again.

"Are you a member of CND?"

"No"

"Who do you know in the peace movement?"

"I don't know what you mean by the peace movement. Do you mean Greenham Common?"

"Who do you know in CND?"

"Lots of my friends are attached to CND."

"Are you a member of the Labour Party?"

"No"

"The Socialist Workers Party?"

"No"

"You do know people in the university in the Socialist Workers Party, don't you?"

"I suppose so."

"Are you a member of the Communist Party?"

"No"

Silence. Steve looked at the ceiling. The round faced man spoke loudly and with evident frustration.

"Look, don't fuck about, what's your interest in the police?"

"It's academic, I think we should all know what's going on."

"Everyone does know what's going on, all you clever lefties are trying to stop free speech, undermine the police and create chaos."

"Tell us about your political interests. Who do you know that's involved in Irish politics?"

Steve sat looking at the man, his political interests weren't even illegal but what would be the point of any kind of discussion with these people. He looked up at the ceiling and for a second he felt tears come to his eyes. They quickly receded.

"All right then, tell us what we already know, tell us about your involvement with the defence campaign?"

"What about your links with Steve Wright and the Police Monitoring Unit?"

The fat faced man almost shouted as he leaned across the table.

"I'm in the defence campaign, if you want to call it that, because a number of my friends were attacked and beaten the night Leon Brittan came, you know. We care about each other."

Steve checked himself. There was no point in wasting finer feelings.

"Steve Wright is just someone who has helped me with my thesis. He's got nothing to do with all this. I've known him for a year or so and he knows a lot about the police. He's irrelevant to this. I only know him through my thesis."

There was complete quiet in the small room, then a vehicle passed beyond the window. He thought about the clear daylight air outside the room. He looked past both men at the far wall, trying to contain his feelings. The two men looked at him. Steve knew that he could last this out, if this was all it entailed.

The round faced man was on the offensive again.

"I think that you're much more involved than you make out. I think you are a left wing organiser, you would describe yourself as that wouldn't you? You think that this society is wrong, you'd like to see it changed. You don't agree with the law do you?"

"Yes" Steve felt a vehemence creep into his voice as he looked at the man's face; then suddenly the questions seemed embarrassingly funny. He smiled.

"You think its funny do you? Do you believe in violence?"

"No"

The round face man stood up determinedly;

"You're not telling us much are you?"

He strode towards the door and left the room, Steve's gaze followed him out.

The pock-marked man leant back in his chair.

"He's very impatient."

He looked at Steve.

"What are you going to do when you leave university?"

"I don't know, it isn't easy to find a job, I'd like to do research."

"I know, unemployment has a lot to do with all these social problems, people get demoralised and have to blame someone. What's it like at university, I suppose money must be a problem?"

"Yes it is"

"Do you prefer living in Manchester or London?"

"London."

"It should be easier to get a job there I would imagine."

Behind him, the door opened again, and when Steve turned his head he saw the balding man half in the room, beckoning the other officer out. They left the room. Steve sat up off his seat slightly and adjusted his clothes. The palms of his hands were sweating, he rubbed them on his trousers. He felt reasonably calm. It crossed his mind that he was about to be released. The two men came back into the room but neither of them sat down.

"We have reason to believe that you are in possession of drugs."

The man with acne stood as if embarassed, his voice wooden and insincere. It was as if he was repeating word for word what someone had told him to say. In the silence Steve stood up.

"Look, are you arresting me or what, I've been here over an

hour and you've said nothing about drugs?''

He had lost his temper; he gathered himself together and said as firmly as he could.

''I want to see a solicitor.''

The bald man stared at him coldly.

''You're not going anywhere and you're not seeing anyone. So just forget it.''

Suddenly the round faced man slapped him across the face hard. Steve tried to steady himself, tried to move with the slap but the heel of the man's hand caught him full on the jaw. Once the cycle of violence began, did it ever stop? Didn't it just go on and on justifying itself? Steve took a deep breath.

''Don't try to be clever''

Again, there was no time to say anything, a heavy push to his chest knocked the breath out of him. The man turned his back. His chest hurt with a deep bruising pain.

''As we suspect you're in possession of drugs, you are required to take your clothes off.''

Now it was beginning. Now he knew that he wasn't going to be let out. This was how it always began. This was when you got beaten and humiliated. It happened when you were naked. The relative comfort of the room would afford him no protection if he was naked. How much resistance could he muster? He had spent hours idly thinking about this kind of situation in other countries while he had been writing his thesis. He had wondered whether people find the courage from within themselves in crisis, or did they break down and become weak.

''What about a doctor? There should be a doctor present.''

He looked at both men in turn. Fat face took a step closer to him again. The taller man just shrugged his wide shoulders and raised his eyebrows slightly.

If he resisted the beating would be greater. He began slowly taking his clothes off. He placed each item of clothing on the table. The pock marked man, sitting at the table, went through each piece like a fetishist, feeling along the linings, checking the seams. Nothing registered on his face. After scrutinising each garment he placed it on a new pile. He took everything out of the trouser pockets and sorted through the contents on the table top.

Steve stood completely naked, trying not to be embarrassed, resisting the temptation to put his hands over his cock; trying to keep his dignity and his strength. The fat faced man had left the room with his clothes and a moment later came back and said something inaudible to the other man. Steve didn't look at either of them. They stood on the opposite side of the table.

"Bend forward onto the table."

He did as the pock marked face man told him. Steve placed his hands on the table as the man walked round it. Was he just going to look up his arse or would it be worse? He tensed himself and then felt a seering pain, he cried out slightly but then clenched his teeth. The pain continued as something was pushed deeper and more probingly up his back passage. He saw the fat faced man stand up from his chair and walk to the door. The pain stopped and he felt the figure behind him move away. The door closed. His arse hurt a lot, he touched it gingerly and found blood on his fingers. He had no idea any longer what he could do, how he could get out of this situation, he felt completely disorientated. He sat down. Instinctively to protect himself, he sat back to front on the chair and faced the door.[73]

It was an hour before anyone entered the room again. Despite the fact that it was well heated, Steve began to shiver and however he sat he couldn't stop the pain in his backside.

The fat faced man came in and put his clothes on the table. He didn't try and reach out for them or put them on. He felt on a knife edge; somehow he simply had to acquiesce in whatever they wanted. The man sat down and stared at him. After a few minutes of silence the pock marked face man came in and the questions began again. The bald man was completely agressive.

"Where were you going when we picked you up?"

And, before he had time to answer;

"Where had you come from?"

Then surprisingly,

"Put your clothes back on."

Perhaps it was a trick, he raised himself slowly from the chair and found his pants on the table. Nothing happened, the two men sat watching him, he pulled on his pants hurredly. Then his trousers. He felt his body relax a little. He pulled up the zip on his flies. The man with the pock marked face spoke casually, in an almost friendly way.

"How did you collect the information for your thesis?"

Steve didn't answer, he continued dressing as if he was considering an answer. He knew that this was the beginning of the real questions.

"I did what people do when they write things, I looked in books and spoke to people who have been involved. Bits of documents I picked up, here and there."

"Are you interested in riots?"

"Academically, I'm interested, how and why they begin; how they are supresssed."

"What do you know about the Moss Side riots in 1981?"

It was all hard to believe, here he was getting dressed in a police station in Manchester while two policemen asked him questions about his thesis material which they had stolen.

"Not much" He felt much more confident now. They had tried to humiliate and disorientate him but when they got to the point he was completely in control of himself.

"How do you think the police were involved?"

Again, he let a long silence pass.

"Sorry, what do you mean, involved?"

"You think the police set them up, don't you?"

Pock face was now trying to have a serious conversation with him. The man stared intelligently at him. The bald headed man got up from his chair and left the room. Steve tried to find an answer which wouldn't offend the officer.

"I think police tactics often create tension and sometimes cause riots, if that's what you mean. I think Scarman[74] thought that as well; it doesn't make me a subversive."

"Would you think that there was any kind of policy to start riots. You would probably think that wouldn't you?"

The tone was amiable again, as if nothing unpleasant had happend in the room.

"No, I wouldn't go as far as that. Who would?"

"Some extreme people seem to think things like that. Some fascist organisations try to do that."

There was silence again. Steve sat down, feeling warmer and more protected with his clothes on. The bald man came back in and stood leaning against the wall.

"You've got your final exams in June. Your finals"

It wasn't a question.

"Yes."

"You don't have to take them. You should worry about your career. You might have to take them a year later. You can sit them a year later can't you?"

"I'm sitting them in June, nothing will stop me. I've finished my thesis."

The round faced man smiled nastily.

"Why did you say that you were burgled."

"Because I was, my thesis material was stolen."

"But the burglary, you were making it up weren't you?"

"No, someone broke into my flat."

"Yes, Top of the Meadow Farm. But you just invented the allegation that your thesis was taken didn't you"

"I didn't make any allegation, I never reported it."

There was a long silence. Was he being told to keep quiet about the burglary. How did you decode the message in all this. Why didn't they just say, "Do this, do that, don't to this, don't do that or else!" It was like playing chess in the dark.

"Think about it, you could fail your exams, you might not even get to take them. We know what course you are on, we know the days of your exams"

"I don't know what you're saying."

Steve tried to work out exactly what the threat was. The bald man continued playing his bizarre game.

"You've already lost your thesis. We have your exam timetable"

"What do you mean, what are you trying to say. Anyway, to some extent, it's all done on continuous assessment. You probably wouldn't understand that"

"Just think about it"

The man with the pock marked face stood up from his chair.

"You can be picked up at any time, day or night, look how easy it was today."

The two men made their way towards the door of the room. Steve sat motionless in the chair.

"You're free to go now, we'll walk along the corridor with you."

The pock marked man opened the door and ushered him through into the corridor. Outside the room, there was noise again, officers walking about talking to each other. All Steve wanted was to get out of the building, reach the fresh air. His arse hurt as he walked.[75] He reached the last outside door and the man with the pock marked face opened it.

"Your car is where you parked it."

"Think about what he said, any time, any place. Goodbye."

He almost ran over to the car. As he got in he looked round for the red Cortina but it had gone. As he drove out through the stone arch he saw it parked half on the pavement and half on the road outside the civilian entrance to the police station. He stopped and wrote down the registration number. Nothing else had been recorded for the last five hours, but he would record that.[76] He drove out into the centre of Manchester, where the world and all its business seemed not to have changed.

Chapter Nine

Fear on the Streets: June—November

Police vigilantism is seldom an overt and never an acknowledged occurrence as far as police authorities are concerned.

Tom Bowden: Beyond the Limits of the Law

For two Manchester students, fear had become an endemic part of their lives. Whatever it was that the police were trying to do to them, it was succeeding; fear produces a sense of impotence in its host. The individual who feels unable to act in freedom, constrained by fear, is trapped, they become subordinate and maleable.

Following his assualt and confinement in Bootle Street police station, Steven Shaw went to see a nurse. He also visited Steve Wright at the monitoring unit, to whom he made a long tape recorded statement and obtained the name of a solicitor. On May 16th, two days after the incident, the solicitor wrote to the Chief Superintendent at Bootle Street. She explained what had happened to Steve and asked for confirmation of the times during which he had been held at the station.

> Would you please confirm the times at which our client was present in Bootle Street police station, and please inform us of the reason for the initial approach by the police and subsequent detention in the police station.

Some time later the solicitor received a phone call apparently from an officer at Bootle Street. He informed her that there was no record of a Steven David Shaw being held at Bootle Street on May 14th. There was however, the policeman said, a Steven David Shaw held at Bootle Street on May 13th. By September 1985, Steven had changed solicitors, his new solicitor wrote again to the GMP asking for further details of the Steven David Shaw who had apparently been taken into Bootle Street the day before his client. He received the following reply:

> I can confirm that your client was arrested on 13th May, 1985 by constable 'D' ********* on suspicion of assault occasioning actual bodily harm. During the course of the investigation, the complainant in the case retracted his allegation and your client was released without charge.

What are we to make of this? There are at least two possible hypotheses. The first is that the information in the letter is completely genuine. Placed in context, however, it appears extremely implausible. Up until the time that Steven was taken to Bootle Street police station, his flat had been burgled, he had been stopped four times for traffic violations and his friends had been placed under surveillance. He was taken to Bootle Street without the visit being recorded and this custody of almost five hours was construed by him as yet another attempt to frighten and intimidate him. Is it likely that another Steven David Shaw was taken to the same station only the day before?[77]

A second hypothesis is that someone was trying to place Steven's custody at Bootle Street at another time and for another offence. If they were doing this, they would obviously not place the incident on the correct day; that would make the coincidence look absurd. Placed as it was the day before his actual custody, it created the impression that Steven was in Bootle Street police station, himself suspected of a serious offence. If this had been the case, could it have been in his interest to lie about his custody? Would the police also be able to claim later that it was on this occasion that Steve had seen the inside of Bootle Street Police Station? It was certainly fortunate for the police that the complainant in this serious offence withdrew his complaint! But perhaps more interesting than all this is the logistics of the apparent arrest. 'D' is the insignia of D division, which includes Longsight police station and the place where Steven was actually stopped by the two plain clothes detectives. It is also the division from which the TAG officers came who policed the demonstration, and Longsight was the station from which the plain clothes detective who infiltrated the crowd came. How did this uniformed 'D' division constable, come to take an arrested man to Bootle Street police station which is in 'A' division?[78]

By the middle of May, following the Bootle Street incident, both Steven and Sarah had been driven to leave Manchester. The only escape from the conspiracy which had chosen them as victims was a physical escape from the imprisoning eyes and ears of the conspirators. Sarah had left England for a period and Steve had returned again to London where he could work in peace on his revision. They both had exams in June.

On the day that Steve had left for London driving not far from Greenheys Lane police station, he had been flashed from behind by a white police Metro. Both officers had got out of the car and walked over. The conversation was very brief, Steven had been accused of speeding but this time had not been asked to produce his documents or issued with an HO/RTI.

By the last week in May, the independent Inquiry set up by Manchester City Council had been publicised and the panel appointed. The last cases of the arrested students were just creeping through the courts, the summer and the examination period was descending upon Manchester. On the day that the final decision to hold the Inquiry was made, and on the following day Sarah Hollis received further anonymous phone calls.

Steven Shaw was so worried and frightened about returning to Manchester that he began negotiations through his tutor to sit his examinations in London. As in all other cases where the University had been approached officially to help either Steven or Sarah, the response was sluggish and inflexible, if not unsympathetic. Steve had been told that he would have to return to Manchester to sit the examinations. The best that the University could do for him was to give him what they considered secure accommodation in the student residences at Whitworth Park. It transpired that this new accommodation was worse than useless because Steven was suddenly thrown into habitation with four second year students whose whole philosophy of life was in opposition to his. For the next three weeks he lived a tense and depressing domestic existence, desperately trying to revise in the midst of loud music and raucous behaviour.

His period at Whitworth Park was not without attention from the police either. The day after his first examination on June 7th he was standing on the pavement outside the student occomodation when a white Sherpa van drew up alongside him. The officer who was driving leaned from the window and said; "Oh, you're living at Whitworth Park now are you?" From that time until the end of his examination on June 20th, he was under constant surveillance from police vehicles parked near his address.

The independent Inquiry was due to have its first hearings in Manchester Town Hall on Saturday and Sunday the 15th and 16th of June. Manchester City Council publicised the event and the press waited eagerly for the first forum. But in the darkness during the week before, others were waiting too. The conspirators must have felt that the objects of their attention were splitting and dividing like a single cell organism. Their strategy needed constant reorganisation to face the new threats. First there was the defence campaign; then followed individual complaints against police officers and their collation under the Avon and Somerset Inquiry; now there was the independent public Inquiry.

On June 11th, four days before the Inquiry sat in Manchester, Sarah Hollis was followed on and off three different buses by a man in civilian clothes. Since returning to Manchester, she had moved to a new address, which she was trying to keep a secret. On June 13th, she returned home to find a white police Sherpa van parked outside her house.

After discussions between Sarah and the Inquiry panel, they had decided that she should give evidence in camera. On Saturday June 15th, she slipped into the Town Hall to meet with the panel, she gave her evidence and left. That evening at nine thirty, she was cycling home after seeing friends, when she was approached by two men who got out of an unmarked red car; she recognised one of them. This time, she faced the sharp end of police culture, a language and a manner of speaking designed to cut deep into the most vulnerable parts of the female identity:

"We've been told that you paid a visit to the Inquiry at the Town Hall today."

Sarah looked from one man to the other while the speaker just stared at her malevolently.

"Been telling them some of your little lies have you?"

There was a pause, then the man added with greater vehemence,

"Well, you can just go back tomorrow and tell them not to take any notice of what you said because you were just lying. Tell them none of it is true, and just remember, we know if you do what we say or not, and if you don't, we'll pay you a little visit in hospital next week."

Sarah was due to go into hospital for the following week and the thought of this and the protection it offered her, made her slightly more assured.

"You won't be allowed in hospital."

One of the men addressing the other began parodying her voice.

"Listen to the clever bitch. If we want to, we can just walk into the Ward M3 female and really give the doctors something to sort out."

Ward M3 was the ward which Sarah was due to stay in and hearing it mentioned brought back her fears; she fell silent.

"Or we could sort something out when she gets out of hospital."

The threats continued as the two men exercised their male power over her.

"Yeah, how do you fancy getting fucked by a black man? You would probably enjoy it because a little bitch like you would never get laid any other time."

The two officers laughed and then asked her if she understood.

"Yes," she answered, she understood very well.

"Well, off you go then, sweetie, and don't try anything clever, because we will find out about it."

They walked away.

With this diatribe of terror, the conspiracy had travelled full circle. Only police officers could organise this kind of sadistic threat; it is not a simple example of random male violence but organised terror with a definite objective. Only police officers inhabit a world of power which educates them in the use of such games. Even violent male criminals rarely have a capacity for such fine and organised control over fear in their victims. On March 1st, police officers had manifested this power against a group of defenceless students; now it was being used to pacify and control a single woman. The logical conclusion in this excercise of absolute power is the system of torture. With this last verbal assault of Sarah, the conspirators had moved onto a new footing. Now the object was evidently not just to intimidate and harass, but to hurt and shatter the identity. On May 15th, a police officer, a presence of the State, had forced his hand inside the body of Steven Shaw. Now they were trying symbolically to enter Sarah Hollis.

The next day Sarah reported everything that had happened to her to the independent Inquiry team at its hotel in the middle of Manchester. She was, though frightened, fighting back. In the week that followed the first sitting of the Inquiry, the press reported the evidence with a surprising degree of objectivity. *The Manchester Evening News* reported; ''Danger of Police Charge'' and the *Guardian,* ''Police Attack Demonstrators Without Warning.'' Meanwhile, shrouded by the secrecy of State agencies, the Avon and Somerset Inquiry persued its own objectives. Officers fell upon people, snatching statements from them, giving bland reassurances and making casual promises of independence and trustworthiness.

On June 20th, Steven Shaw finished his examinations and returned immediately to the home of his parents in London[79]. Relief at having finished his exams was soon overtaken by the need for a job. The pressure from the conspiracy was off for as long as he stayed in London and began to live a different kind of life. Although its tentacles still reached out to find him, their power was diluted. Apart from intercepted mail, a death threat in the form of an unstamped letter pushed under the door of his new place of work, and one telephone call in which an anonymous male told him he 'was dead', his life settled into an orderly routine[80]. It would be another seven months before he was again thrown into conflict with the forces of the conspiracy.

Both Sarah and Steve had, it seemed, struggled through the worst parts of their personal nightmare, and emerged with their identities intact. By the middle of June they had shifted the weight from their own shoulders onto those of socially responsible individuals within the council and on the Inquiry panel.

In 1985, Tony Bunyan was the Adviser to the Greater London Council Police Committee, head of a large police committee support unit. An academic and an activist liked and respected by the left, he was pleased to accept a place offered him on the Inquiry panel. On the evening of June 25th, just over a week after the panel's first sitting in Manchester, Tony was making his way back to his sixth floor office after a long meeting. County Hall, with its labyrinth of corridors, was in half darkness and almost deserted.

As he neared his office door, he heard it close and then the quick footfalls of someone in a hurry. He made his way to the office with slight trepidation. Inside the office everything appeared to be in order but then, when he looked more closely, he saw that his notebook of the Inquiry hearings had gone.

On the following morning, June 26th staff returned to the Manchester Police Monitoring Unit where all the documents of the Inquiry were being held, to find that that too had been entered. Conveniently, and as a token to a more respectable criminality, the burglars had taken one pound. Notebooks, papers and files had all been disturbed.

Three weeks later, on July 19th, there was a burglary at the home of Ann Lewis, one of the workers at the Police Monitoring Unit in Manchester; she had been working informally as a clerk to the Inquiry panel. Again, nothing of any significance was missing but her papers and documents relating to the Inquiry had been interfered with.

On July 22nd, both the *Guardian* and the *Manchester Evening News* carried full reports of the harassment of both Steve and Sarah. Reporters on the *Guardian* in particular believed that its authoritative and liberal voice would still or at least constrain the pattern of violence which the two students had so far been subjected to.

At the end of July 1985, during what appeared, at least publicly, to be a lull in the activities of the conspiracy, Steven Shaw saw members of the independent Inquiry panel in London. Gradually, as the story of these two haunted individuals began to materialise, the panel decided to make the information public.

The present period in this country is characterised not only by thuggery from the right at the base of society, reinforced by vicious legislation from the top, but also by a liberal desire from the centre to believe that even the worst of our political problems can be resolved by reasoned argument. Liberal workers in the media still maintain an implicit belief in their power to mediate social conflicts and exert pressure on agents and agencies of the State to listen and reform. In October 1985, the publication of the report of the independent Inquiry by Manchester City Council was followed by immediate media attention[81].

On October 31st, the BBC 'Brass Tacks' programme featured the policing of the student demonstration at the University. The research team spent some time with Steve and Sarah before deciding not to include film of their harassment in the programme. Although the programme had begun as a defence of the students, it ended up as a speculative discourse on the origins and development of riot policing. Although the programme gave exposure to the case of the students arrested, it left them with no protection. On November 7th, 'Out of Court' transmitted a detailed appraisal of Steven and Sarah's predicament, but this held out no more powerful protection for either of them than had other publicity.

James Anderton remained quiet in public following the publication of the Inquiry report but his Deputy Chief Constable, John Stalker, was quick to make a statement in the form of a letter to the 'Out of Court' programme. In November, he rejected the findings of the Inquiry and introduced the visit of another tory member of parliament, later in the year, to support his assertion that there were violent people in the University[82].

Chapter Ten

Fear on the Streets: November—February

Policemen turn to vigilantism on occassions as an act of self-preservation where they feel their lives or their jealously guarded authority to be at stake.

Tom Bowden: Beyond the limits of the Law.

The original brief of the Avon and Somerset investigation had been quite explicit; they were to enquire into the policing of the student demonstration on March 1st. and investigate complaints against any police officers. It was the police who were the subject of this investigation and it was being carried out on behalf of complainants, those who were victims of police misbehaviour on the night. A large number of the students, particularly the activists, believed from the beginning that this investigation was simply a damage limitation exercise. The investigation had been set in train simply to quiet public indignation at the use of new police tactics in public order situations.

The students' scepticism focused upon two issues; firstly it was common knowledge that if you made an official complaint against the police there was a chance that you would bring down even more harassment upon yourself. Secondly, people knew that however competently the Avon and Somerset officers carried out their investigation, it was a paper exercise. Like all similar investigations which had preceded it, from the Times inquiry through to Countryman, it could only be a structural examination. It would ultimately be impossible to conduct an enquiry into what was institutionally rotten in the police force because basic tenets of power and democracy would have to be questioned. Even if an enquiry did not penetrate as deeply as this, aspects of police culture reflecting innate power relations such as sexism, racism and anti-socialism would have to be examined.

Officers from Avon and Somerset had already shot themselves in the foot when they handed over statements taken from the students to the Greater Manchester Police prosecuting solicitors. Deputy Chief

Constable Reddington had reinforced his 'impartiality' by raising his voice to Sarah Hollis in response to her tentative suggestion that the police might be harassing her. He had also spoken unequivocally to Ann Lewis when discussing the night on the steps; "You will just have to get used to this kind of policing." Any lingering hopes of a competent and independent investigation were blown apart by the unreasoned denials which met the publication of the facts indicating that Greater Manchester Police officers were carrying on an organised war of attrition against witnesses.

Somewhere in the collective mind of the Avon and Somerset investigation, these reports overloaded the system and a fuse blew. From then on, the logic of the investigation would continually short circuit and be overtaken by a kind of lunatic overdrive. By the time the *Guardian* published the detailed accounts of the harassment of Steven Shaw, there could have been few police officers in the Greater Manchester Area, visitor or resident, who were willing to work with an open mind and bring any conspirators to justice. Even normally trustworthy 'moles' inside the Greater Manchester force began to parrot an official line, that it was the students who were conspirators and not the police. A strange sub-plot began to develop in the case. Why had Steven Shaw not reported the break in, or his five hour ordeal in police custody, to the police? Anyone who was not a police officer could answer this question with a fairly simple objective logic, but police officers suddenly suffering from imaginative amnesia began to chant them like incantations which held vital evidence to the meaning of life itself.

Now the victim and the detective began to inhabit different realities. The fact that Steven Shaw had not reported these incidents to the people who had been involved in them, meant not only that he did not trust the police, but that he was a subversive. Together with others, Steven Shaw was trying to undermine the State and the morale of the police force by propaganda and misinformation. Both he and Sarah Hollis were building fantasies which rode into battle against the State. Ghosts in the steel city.

Avon and Somerset officers were not going to investigate fantasies, after all their investigation had already cost nearly a quarter of a million pounds. They began to work energetically on a process of policing in reverse, they set out to *disprove* the stories of both Sarah

Hollis and Steven Shaw.

In August, Avon and Somerset officers approached Steven's professor at Manchester University. They made enquiries about his thesis and his thesis material; they asked what kind of student he was and how capable he had been of finishing his thesis. Here began a battle for the reality of Steven Shaw's case, a battle which would only be resolved when police officers had captured all the witnesses to the events after March 1st, and persuaded them to collude in *their* reality as against that of the twenty three year old student.

Somehow, they had to persuade Steven to see them; they had to extract his story from him in order to disassemble it; to disprove it, they had to know it in every detail. The University authorities, though sympathetic to the Avon and Somerset investigation, could not put pressure on Steven and they continued to withold his London address. But by November, officers were in contact with his solicitor. They began a slow process of attrition, by reason and by threat, to wear down both Steven's and his solicitor's policy of not making a formal complaint.

Meanwhile, Sarah Hollis, who had begun with complete faith in the Avon and Somerset officers and their investigation, was now mistrustful and cynical. She was trying to move away from the whole problem, to tackle it on another plane. She determinedly resisted any constraint upon her life which organised protection would inevitably have entailed. She confused and angered Manchester City Council officers by her steadfast view that she had to live her life and not be intimidated[83]. But deep behind this strength, other ideas could be seen struggling to the surface. If the problem was simply ignored, perhaps it would go away.

On November 15th, just a week after the transmission of the 'Out of Court' programme, Sarah was followed around central Manchester by two men in civilian clothes, one of whom she recognised from a previous encounter. Then suddenly, in the light of the early evening, the two men accosted her. They jostled her, pushed her from one to the other, and threatened her with rape. One of them sexually assaulted her, putting his hand inside her coat.

For Sarah, the situation was now becoming critical. Always in two minds about whom she could trust, acutely aware of her vunerability as a woman, she began to inhabit a twilight world where only a very few close friends were told of what was happening.

Throughout December a cold respite descended over the activities of the conspiracy. By now there were fewer threats for the conspirators to consider. The independent Inquiry report had come and gone, together with all the media coverage that Manchester City Council could muster; it presented no more threat to the police than it provided protection for the students. Only Sarah had spoken to the Avon and Somerset officers; if Sarah withdrew her complaint the conspirators could rest easy.

Steven stayed in London, making occasional trips to Manchester to visit friends; both he and the conspirators knew that these visits were not connected with any complaint. However, by the middle of January, Avon and Somerset officers had almost persuaded Steven and his solicitor to make a formal statement about everything which had happened to him since March 1st. 1985.

On January 15th, at eight in the evening, Sarah Hollis left a house in Rusholme where she had spent a pleasant evening with friends. In the light of the street lamps, as she stepped from the front door onto the pavement, she saw two men. She recognised one of them as a man who had threatened her previously. She turned and ran back into the house and the protection of her friends. Would the nightmare ever go away?

Two days later, again in the evening, Sarah cycled to Monsall Hospital. For part of her journey she was aware of a marked white police car following slowly in her wake. Further on she came upon it parked by the pavement in front of her. She cycled past, trying to retain her courage. The car window was open; she stared straight ahead, not taking her eyes off the road. As she passed, the quiet voice of a single uniformed officer ebbed behind her.

"She has just passed now."

Violent Sunday

By the end of the third week of January 1986, Steven Shaw had been out of Manchester for eight months. The fear and the intrigue of the previous year were beginning to leave him. Settling into his job with a research project in Clerkenwell, his degree safely behind him, the last year might have to be put down to experience.

He had played his part in both the defence campaign and the Manchester City Council public Inquiry. The matter of his assault in Bootle Street police station was now with his London solicitors, who were preparing a civil action for damages against the Greater Manchester Police.

Steve believed implicitly in resolving the questions raised by his harassment in a public and political way, through the press, through political organisation and through the courts. He had no faith in the Avon and Somerset investigation. Since the previous July, however, officers working from publicity about his case had been trying to get access to him. Unlike many of the other students that the Avon and Somerset team had interviewed, Steve was now no longer isolated. He was surrounded, and to some extent protected, not only by the publicity that the 'Out of Court' television programme and newspaper coverage afforded him but by his solicitor and a group of concerned individuals from the public Inquiry and the Police Monitoring Unit[84].

By November 1985, having made little headway in their attempts to speak to Steven through the University, detectives were concentrating their efforts on his London solicitor. Steve stuck steadfastly to the policy of non-co-operation adopted by the Students Union. His solicitor, working upon his client's instructions, consistently informed

Avon and Sumerset that Steven did not wish to co-operate and that they were taking an action for damages over his custody in Bootle Street.

In all cases of this kind, resisting the pressure to comply with the police becomes a trial of strength. The whole weight of the system encourages the solicitor and his client to trust to accepted procedure; yet a more combatative and radical consciousness tells activists to work outside the system and then use the courts against the police. Interwoven with this essentially political question is a technical and legal question. Despite protestations of independence on the part of investigating police officers, information given in connection with a formal police complaint might well be used against the complainant in any related court case. In this struggle to gain possession of the witnesses, reason and persistence are on the side of the detective.

Steve and his solicitor began with their faces set against the onslaught of frequent phone calls and visits from Avon and Somerset officers. By January, their resistance was beginning to crumble. Advice about the use of the complaints system and the need to complain formally before taking a civil action began to hold sway. By the third week in January, a date had been set for Steve to meet Avon and Somerset officers and make a detailed statement about the Brittan visit and his subsequent harassment.

On Wednesday January 22nd, detectives Stribley and Williams travelled from Somerset and met Steven and his solicitor in the solicitor's office off High Holborn. The meeting began tentatively, but gradually as some kind of trust was established, Steven made a start on a statement. When finally completed, the statement was fifty eight pages long and had taken eighteen hours of writing to resolve.

For Steve, relating the past year's harassment was a gruelling, emotional and tiring experience. It returned him to the scene of his conflicts and reimmersed him in the emotional sea of isolation and fear that he had suffered in Manchester. The last session which began late on the Thursday night did not finish until 2.40am on Friday. The statement was a massively detailed document, particularly where it concerned police officers. On the instructions of his solicitor, Steve had refused to name friends who might have supported his statement until he had himself spoken to them and found out whether they would be willing to co-operate.

When Steven left the offices of his solicitor at 3.00am, he was tired and disorientated. He had smoked too many cigarettes and the dirty business of recounting his harassment stuck to his skin like a grimy film. Stribley and Williams, no doubt equally tired, had insisted at the end that the whole matter could only really be tied up if they obtained contributory statements from the people Steve had refused to name. In fact, these witnesses could add nothing to Steven's allegations about police officers, who were the ones Avon and Somerset officers should have been investigating. That Avon and Somerset officers were so keen to see Steven's friends adds weight to the theory that they were actually testing the veracity *of his statement*, not trying to find the police officers responsible.

Principally there were three people who Steve would have to see and he agreed to consider travelling to Manchester to see if they were willing to talk with Avon and Somerset officers. Yes, he probably would go to Manchester next week, but now he was tired, he just wanted to go home and sleep.

Over the weekend he firmed up his plans to take time off work and travel to Manchester. He contacted friends by phone and arranged to arrive on Thursday on the early evening train. Although he sensed that Manchester was not a place for him to be, he had already made a number of trips and the visit held no special fear for him. All that was to change when he arrived and talked to the staff of the Manchester Police Monitoring Unit.

Steve travelled with a friend for security. As they left the platform at Manchester Piccadilly they noticed a group of uniformed police officers standing on the concourse watching the ticket barrier. They took a taxi from the station to the house of Steve's woman friend; one of a row of small square red brick houses in Rushford Street, Longsight. The streets in the area intersected at right angles, while each row of houses had an alley running down the back. The front doors of the houses opened immediately onto the pavement and the red brick created a desolate but ordered inner city atmosphere.

The house, occupied by four women, two students and two at work, had a pleasant airy atmosphere. Steven's first visitor was Ann Lewis from the police monitoring unit; the story which she had to tell him should have radically altered his behaviour while he stayed in Manchester.

At about eight o'clock on the previous evening, Sarah Hollis had left Dulcie High School where she had been doing circuit training; unusually she had gone alone. She collected her cycle and pushed it along the curb outside the school with her foot, while she did up her coat and put on her gloves. She switched the front light on then reached backwards to turn on the back light. When she turned back, a man was standing astride the front wheel of her cycle.

Another man moved from behind him to stand silently behind her; a classic police manouvre, when two detectives stop a single person; the one officer moving behind to cut off her escape route. She recognised the man in front of her as the same man who had spoken to her on Saturday June 15th, when he was driving a red car, and who had spoken to her and pushed his hand inside her coat on November 15th 1985.

The man at the front said;

''Here's that little whore again.''

He began shouting abuse at her and before she could think what to do, he punched her hard in the face. The force of the blow threw her backwards; she was pushed forwards again by the second man into another punch which landed on her right eye. Sarah and her cycle began to fall towards the pavement. She managed to right herself and though she couldn't see properly began to cycle away.

After telling Steve about Sarah, Ann Lewis advised him not to leave his friends' house alone. The City Council was willing to provide him with any protection or security that he asked for.

That Thursday Steve stayed in all evening. The house now appeared small and claustrophobic. The following day he made what arrangements he could on the phone, asking those whom he wanted to see to visit him. The day dragged and Steve inevitably felt cooped up. Early in the evening he succumbed to the temptation of fresh air and decided to walk alone round the corner and up an ajoining street to the off-licence to buy wine for an evening meal.

Outside it was cold. There were still people about in the streets although it was almost dark, a few young Asian children ran about in a group shouting and laughing. Steve walked across Rushford Street and turned the first corner[85]. As he walked, he periodically glanced over his shoulders, as worry and paranioa had taught him to do. For a brief second he saw two men appear round the corner behind him;

almost shadows, then they stood back and were gone. But the shadows stayed imprinted on his mind. One of the figures was tall and the other shorter; they both seemed to have overcoats on. These images were like parts of a dream. They had reason to appear; at the same time, they were insubstancial. He quickened his pace and reached the off-licence. On his return journey he saw nothing.

On Saturday he again sat round the house. He saw one of his witnesses and asked if they would be willing to give evidence to the Avon and Somerset investigation. He watched television. The occupants of the house came and went as on an ordinary winter Saturday; shopping, getting ready and going out in the evening. Steve went to bed early after watching television. He began to wonder what his life was coming to; was this the price you paid for being politically involved? He lay on the bed and looked at the walls. He heard cars on the road outside, people talking, the steps of heels on the flagstones. How long would his life continue like this.

Sunday was a much slower day. The people in the house had a common friend who lived a few streets away, February 2nd. was his birthday. In the early afternoon everyone left the house to go to the local pub. There was a long discussion about whether or not it was safe for Steve to accompany them; sensible paranoia won the day. When the front door had shut, leaving a trail of voices in the house, Steve sat down and began watching television.

Time dragged, he smoked and drank coffee, then he ran out of cigarettes and he fancied some chocolate. The off-licence was only two streets away, it was a bright Sunday afternoon and he was miles from anywhere; the police had never been particularly active round here. He put on a jacket, checked his keys and stepped out of the house.

Funny how quiet Sundays can be, odd that such a peculiar institution can exist for so long, despite the need to produce, to buy and to sell. It had rained some hours before, the road and the pavement were still wet; it was chilly. He crossed the road and turned right into the next street. To anyone observing him, he wouldn't have appeared to have any particular purpose as he ambled along.

The short road was deserted, the launderette closed. In houses along the road, bits and pieces of other people's lives came into contact with Steven Shaw. A man going to his car, a woman changing the curtains. He didn't see them, but they saw him. There was a large skip near the end of the road, full to overflowing with rubbish and bits of broken houses[86].

As he came level with the skip, it happened with a flurry of coats, faces and fists. Two men charged him, he was thrown back almost off his feet into the alley between the backs of the houses, then dragged along. He hit the alley wall with a thump and his eyes just focused on the two figures. Instantly he recognised them, one with acne down the side of his face, the other balding and slightly older. No words were spoken. The first blow hit him glancingly on the side of the face. He lifted his arm and plunged his fist forward, it caught one of the men square in the mouth which jolted his arm, but then they were crowding him; they were on him.

He didn't feel the blows as they rained on his face, it was just a dazzle of small pains and a blurr of skin. The blows kept coming, about ten in all and by this time he was out of the fight, just a punch bag, kept on his feet by the rough brick wall. One of the men was holding a glass bottle under his arm and he began to swing this at Steve's midrift. The other kept punching, now to the chest and stomach. Within the few seconds that this took to happen, Steve gave up; he didn't think, he just waited. Then he was on the dirt floor of the alley, a foot struck him in the back and then the head. For a second there was nothing, he rolled over and looked up, his eyes out of focus, his head spinning.

One of the men was on his haunches, only a couple of feet before him, it was the man with the pock marked face. Was he going to kill him? A hand came up before his eyes, it held a cigarette, he felt a breath blow over his face and it glowed red. It was only inches in front of his eyes, he could feel the heat of it and smell the smoke. it seemed almost to be burning his retina. It dipped slightly and he felt a dull pain as it burnt the flesh of his cheek bone. Then the unfocused heat before his eye again, then the burning. Once again the cigarette tipped and burnt him.

Over the pain, somewhere beyond his unfocusable eyes, out of the pink face, the mouth moved. ''Don't tell!'' The voice lingered with the pain as he watched the backs of the two men walk slowly away from him. For a second he closed his eyes, then quickly opened them. He was on the edge of unconsciousness; he had to get back to the white rooms, the small house, his friends. He raised himself and fell staggering across the road, he didn't look anywhere, just concentrated on keeping on his feet. Across the road he kept along the wall clinging to it like a man blind drunk. He tumbled along the next road and then fell onto the step of his house. His body was numb and painful at intervals, he trawled around in his pocket mechanically for the key and opened the door. Inside he slammed the door and almost ran into the kitchen.

The fear coursed through him. He had no idea whether it was over. He wanted to leave the house and run but how and where to? In the kitchen he searched for a weapon, his hand fell on a rolling pin. Now the pain was pushing aside the numbness, he staggered back down the hall way, slumped against the wall and sat jammed across the bottom of the door, the rolling pin in his hand. he lost consciousness.

Chapter Eleven

Hunting Ghosts

Now everything's a little upside down,
As a matter of fact, the wheels have stopped,
What's good is bad, What's bad is good,
You find out when you've reached the top
You're on the bottom.

Bob Dylan: Idiot Wind

The attack on Steven Shaw on Sunday February 2nd, by the same two men who had held and assaulted him in Bootle Street police station, was as serious in intent as it could have been. He was lucky to be alive. How might the police have responded to this serious crime in any other circumstances? An immediate and detailed statement, matched with the description already given to Avon and Somerset officers, could have provided them with substancial evidence. Identikit pictures made while Steve was in hospital would have provided an important investigative aid. Quite obviously the two men did not simply come across Steve, they must have been waiting in the area for some time, probably in a car. It is highly unlikely that they were on their own, there must have been back-up surveillance from at least two other men for them to be in position. An immediate house to house enquiry could have gathered a mass of information for the police to work on. Steve had managed to land a hard blow on the face of one of his assailants, so hard that his knuckles had been bruised; here was further evidence of indentification. Of course, it was of no use at all, if the police decided that this was simply a random attack by unknown civilians; if they suspected even faintly that the assailants were police officers, it was of great value. In fact if they imagined that the men were police officers, a quick routine check on Longsight and Greenheys Lane police stations would have told them where all the plain clothes officers were on duty. Neither Avon and Somerset officers nor any officers from the Greater Manchester Police took any of these steps.

The attack had to be turned into a crime that never happened.

There would be no posters on the buses and police notice boards, asking for the public to help the police with their enquiries. There would be no appeals on regional news programmes with identikit pictures. There would be no observation of officers as they next appeared for duty at Longsight, Greenheys Lane or Bootle Street police stations. There would be no circulation of identikit pictures to any of these stations. There would be no identikit pictures *at all* until a desultory two weeks had passed, and there would be no house to house enquiries for a week. Then, even this would be a charade, carried out simply to make it appear that something was being done.

A short time after his arrival in hospital Avon and Somerset officers were at his bedside. The next day Steven was taken to London in a private ambulance hired by his solicitor. When Steven Shaw left Manchester Royal Infirmary, the first person he saw on his way out was a Greater Manchester Police officer. The Greater Manchester Police had been called in by his solicitor to protect him.

A week before Steven had travelled to Manchester, he had given a statement to Avon and Somerset officers for the first time. Police officers in Manchester were obviously aware of this and it had radically changed their ground plan for dealing with their own defence. Steven had gone to Manchester at the wishes of Avon and Somerset officers, to speak to witnesses. Somehow the conspiracy, the criminals about whom Avon and Somerset officers should have been gaining evidence, knew his plans in detail.

The attack in February galvanised those who had been associated with Steven's and Sarah's cases into more coherent action. Now, it was completely obvious what was going on. As the days passed after February 2nd, and no one was caught, it became clear that this last attack was not going to be placed within the context of the year long series of incidents. With the help of lawyers in London and the closer involvement of Steven's parents, together with the complete commitment of Manchester City Council, a new strategy for the case was resolved.

Firstly it was decided to give maximum media coverage to the latest attack and the year long campaign of harassment[87]. Secondly, investigators began work on following up every lead and every incident which had taken place over the previous year. Now, for the first time, a number of experienced people were about to take the whole matter out of the hands of the police and begin an investigation.

The forces were polarised. It was almost a full year since Avon and Somerset officers had begun their investigation and the same period had passed since the burglary of Steven's flat. From early in their investigation, Avon and Somerset officers had been trying to disprove rather than prove Steven and Sarah's accounts of harassment. The new and energetic investigation, completely outside the auspices of the police, could only be viewed as a threat to the credibility of Avon and Somerset officers.

The conspiracy must have realised that the new investigation was also a threat to them, though how much of the threat they couln't know. But now their focus had to change; information had been passed on from the original two victims to a small number of specialists, most of whom were beyond fear and protected from the physical threats that had been made against the two students. While the conspiracy had to keep the new investigation under observation, they had become unsafe and exposed. All they could do was hope that the sordid work they had done in threatening and harassing witnesses would pay off.

The independent investigators soon found that whenever a witness who might help substanciate Steven's story was located, Avon and Somerset officers had spoken to them. Some witnesses had been approached twice, once by Avon and Somerset officers, the second time by officers of the Greater Manchester police.

In April 1986, Sarah Hollis received another threat from the men who had previously attacked her. It was the final straw and she decided to drop her complaint against the Greater Manchester Police for any previous harassment. Steve was now almost completely isolated and in media terms, the story was getting old. In June 1986, the Avon and Somerset report was sent first to the Police Complaints Authority and then, almost immediately, to the Director of Public Prosecutions. Some weeks before that, Avon and Somerset officers had returned to their own constabulary, leaving Greater Manchester Police officers in 'Y' Department, the complaints branch, to handle any queries or further evidence against their own officers in the matter of the attack on Steven Shaw.

On the day that the Avon and Somerset report reached the Police Complaints Authority, the Deputy Chief Contable of Greater Manchester and the head of the GMP Special Branch, John Stalker, who had overseen the Avon and Somerset Inquiry for the Manchester Police, was suspended. There were few tears shed on his behalf by those associated with the Steven Shaw case when it was later speculated that he had become the victim of an attempt to cover up an internal police investigation which he headed.

The first part of the Avon and Somerset report to the P.C.A. advised some disciplinary actions against a few of the officers who had been present on the steps of Manchester University Students Union on March 1st. The second part unpicked and attempted to disprove the story of Steven Shaw, and invited the Director of Public Prosecutions to consider prosecuting him for wasting police time.

Chapter Twelve

The Victim Reborn

But this secrecy has become a god in this country, and those people who have secrets travel in a kind of fraternity and they will not speak to anyone else.

Senator J. William Fulbright,
Chairman, US Senate Foreign Relations Committee.

Accountability: Power and Reality

The State apparatus works in a bizarre and Kafkaesque manner. In June 1986, over a year after the visit of Leon Brittan to Manchester University Students Union, the Avon and Somerset investigation tendered their report. Within a week it had been referred by the Complaints Authority to the Director of Public Prosecutions. The instigation of that inquiry, its slow progress and its final submission might, at first sight, appear to represent some logical search after truth. The fact is however, that from its beginning in the incident on the steps, the matter was all, 'an affair of State' and no information from official sources has reached the public domain.

It is ironic, or perhaps predictable, that the Home Secretary's visit to Manchester University to give a talk on 'Law and Order' should provoke one of the most serious outbreaks of police disorder over the last few years. That an inquiry should then be conducted by a police force of which the Home Secretary is the administrative head is even more bizarre.

The Avon and Somerset report will represent the official reality of what happened on the night of March 1st 1985, and it will draw official conclusions about the assault and harassment of students following Brittan's visit. Many of those students who gave statements may think now that it was never a search for the truth but a highly partisan exercise in propaganda.

The official propaganda campaign relies upon a number of tactics to secure its aim. By taking its time, it destroys the symbolic coherence of events; by the time any action is taken the immediate reality of the incident will have been diffused; the clear link between actions and justice, always dependent upon immediacy for effect, will be broken by a confusion of other stories and facts pushed into the public mind. In this particular case the Education Bill came before the Lords and 'freedom of speech' for government Ministers became an issue; there were changes in the public order law and television news programmes showed film of student violence at Manchester University; James Anderton pursued his ceaseless criticism of the Labour council and asked for riot training centres, public disorder following Brittans' visit being cited as proof of the need for such facilities.

While the State confuses simple issues and diffuses their coherence, the police on the ground weave a cocoon of myth and subjective prejudice around events. It is this myth which permeates the police force. It percolates through casual talk in canteens and cars and is spread to friends outside the force. It is a version of events which is easily believed by police officers because it avoids any examination of their own corporate behaviour. The more extravagant the behaviour of the police, the more bizarre is the myth woven around it.

In the case of Steven Shaw the myth of his harrassment has evolved slowly, and has grown to proportions which do justice to the Brothers Grimm. As with all rumour, it cannot be fought in a court of law, it cannot even be publicly refuted, because it is the censure of private justice wrought by the police using their own prevailing cultural network.

It might be said that myth and rumour have a sound basis in reality; the reality of subconscious fear. A myth is the collective expression of the deepest fears felt by its originators. The story which follows is based upon things said to different people by either the Avon and Somerset officers or officers of the Greater Manchester Police.

There was a need to give maximum security to the Home Secretary on his visit to the University because no one could be sure whether the IRA might not take the opportunity of the visit to assassinate him. The demonstration organised by extremists on the hard left was a cover to attack Leon Brittan and destroy the right to free speech. The Greater Manchester Police had negotiated Brittan's entry into the building with the students, through the front doors, and half an hour before the visit they began to clear the steps. They asked students in a polite and reasonable way to move but they met fierce resistance in the form of a large number of students who physically attacked them. They were unaware that the doors at the top of the steps were locked.

Students who were prominent in the demonstration were checked by the Special Branch and a number of them targetted as being particularly dangerous. After the demonstration, various of these students conspired together, possibly with the help of radical journalists and professional agitators, to undermine the morale of the police and to discredit them. One primary way in which they decided to do this was to propagate a number of lies about police harassment. Steven Shaw was a hard line political activist and subversive who had contact with a number of people on the left involved in activities aimed at undermining the State, from Irish politics to police monitoring. In particular Shaw had decided to do his thesis on police technology and this interest marked him from the beginning as a subversive.

Although he later claimed that his flat was burgled, and his thesis material stolen, there was no evidence for this. In fact he told a number of different stories to different people before he decided to tell the newspapers, months later, that he suspected the police. The most likely truth is that, because he was behind in his work and unable to finish his thesis, he took the opportunity to claim he had been burgled in order to discredit the police.

Steven Shaw was never at Bootle Street, or, if he had been there, it was at some time before he claimed, perhaps when he was writing his thesis. The room in which he claims he was questioned does not actually exist in the way that he describes it. No police officer would ever take a person into custody without first booking them in and reporting the custody to the desk sergeant. The force rules on this are so strict that a police officer could not get away with it. Again, a long time elapsed before be reported that he had been held and given an internal body search. He chose again to report this to symphtetic journalists rather than to the police.

If Steven Shaw has had injuries to his anus, if he has had to have operations, then it is clear how he got the injuries. He is a known homosexual and his injuries are commensurate with injuries caused by homosexual intercourse. The operations which he has had were, anyway, not for a rupture but for 'anal syphilis.'

There is no evidence the Steven Shaw was ever stopped for speeding and at no time was he summonsed to appear before a court. It seems remarkable that on each of these occasions when he says he was stopped that he was alone and there were therefore no witnesses. Although Steven Shaw received some injuries on February 2nd 1986, this day was a Sunday and the area where he says he was attacked was completely deserted; consequently there were no witnesses. The police do not believe that Shaw was actually attacked, or that he was on route to the off-licence. It is clear that not only is he a homosexual but that he delights in sado-masochistic practices. He was indulging in these on that day somewhere in the area near his friends' house. In fact, he had specifically left the house and was out 'cottaging' in the area. He burnt his own face with a cigarette. A consultant would give evidence that the burns are too regular and close to each other to have been administered during a struggle, by another person. He later blamed the attack upon the police, conveniently trying it in with the two mysterious people who he says took him to Bootle Street.

The red Ford Cortina, which Shaw says stopped him and directed him to Bootle Street police station if it exists at all, does not belong to Greater Manchester Police, nor is it owned by any of their officers privately.

Sarah Hollis, it is understood, has withdrawn any complaint against the police, and this goes to show that she now knows that police officers were not involved. Although journalists got a young man called Frank Logan to say that he had been put up to burgling her flat by the police, he was paid to say this by the journalists. In fact, this young man is a petty crook who would say anything for money; he too is a homosexual whom the Vice Squad have been trying to catch for some time. Amanda Hughes, the young woman with whom Frank Logan committed the burglary, has made a long statement to the police explaining how journalists tried to pressure her into saying that the police put her up to the burglary.

In this case, we once again find ourselves up against the wall over the issue of accountability. No external structure of accountability could break through the cultural hegemony of a large institution which conspires to commit criminal acts and then has the power to disseminate such myths. Lies are not simply negations of truth but bricks in the building of a serparate and different reality.

The police force is now almost an autonomous power, a separate institution. Its organisation exists and is nurtured by the continuity of its own culture and its own myth. That myth and that culture is spreading out to become the prevalent or dominant mode of reality in the broader society. It is not possible to diffuse and disassemble the *police reality* because the State and all its agencies ensure that it has a greater symbolic significance than the reality presented in atomised and shattered form by less powerful individuals in the broader society.

The culture of the police can only be changed by changing their social relations and their relationship as a whole to the structure of power and control in society. In turn this has to be done by taking away their actual physical power in the world, while at the same time demystifying their symbolic representation. This can not be done until another view of the world gains control of the means of representation, and a new ideology becomes prevalent.

Accountability: The point of impotence

When we investigate the crimes of State agencies, we cannot expect to come to solutions which are logical within our reality. More than this, individuals and campaigning organisations have to acknowledge the 'point of impotency.' To continue investigating cases beyond this point and to still retain a belief in individual, rather than corporate or class justice, is to blind oneself to the fact that we are dealing with a political process not individual moral culpability.

This point of impotency might be called the 'Murell Factor.'[88] It is reached and can be recognised when all the logic of detection, the continuity of act and causation, comes to a crumbling halt; when reason is disassembled by propaganda and ideology. Throughout the Steven Shaw case, the investigators came up against this blinding irrationality not only from the police but from many others, who either had a stake in the State, or were cowed by the power of the State. When I wrote an article for the *New Statesman*, I was asked to change a sentence which stated that Steven Shaw was attacked by the same two *police officers* who had taken him to Bootle Street police station. I insisted that they were police officers; they had shown Steven warrant cards and they took him to a police station. They might, I was told, be 'friends of police officers' or 'members of right wing groups who were close to the police'. As Ann Lewis said when I told her this; "Yes and they might have built a cardboard replica of Bootle Street and taken him there."

Only those who have a vested interest in the State would try to destroy the evidential reality of the world within which the victim lives. People *might* fall down steps inside police stations. People *might* bang their heads against walls. People *might* punch themselves in the face. Most racial attacks *might* be carried out by their victims. People *might* manufacture stories about rape and internal body searches to cover deep malfunctioning within their own internal world. However, the *probability* is that an agent other than the victim has inflicted injuries in these cases.

When reason, probability, evidence, logic and the victim themselves tells the investigator that something happened and only the State or its agents tells us that it didn't, it is time to shut the book and consider the case proven. Retribution and justice will only be obtained after the political process has transferred power from the State to those who have been historically denied it.

None of this means that we should not embark upon such investigations. The very process of investigation itself helps us to build and educate those who have need of resisting the State and its violence. We learn continually more about the State and its organisation and during this difficult education we organise our defence against it. As long as *we link our social investigation with political action* we are still on course for change.

The specific conclusions to this book and its story are inconclusive. But would anything have been resolved if one or two particular officers were brought before the court, and even (miraculously) convicted; would this advance our understanding of, or our own organisation against, the political processes which nurture the State? In all probability it would only further legitimise a process of law and policing which is bent upon destroying any dissent.

The political lessons in this case are the important ones. So it would seem only right that we draw these here; that our investigators are not left to ride off into the urban sunset with easy consciences. The investigator, like the policemen, who sees every case as a separate incident, who ignores the social matrix of the offence, has no politics. This lack of politics is in itself a political perspective which upholds the society within which these offences are commonplace. For the investigator who believes in political lessons, there can never be the neat ending of one case and the beginning of another. Thre can only be an analysis built upon years of cases which prove a political direction and which help us change the world in which we live, so that these offences are less common.

Accountability: The Grave Diggers

Much of the story between the lines of this book is about the search for public justice within a system which has been privatised by those who control the State. The State in capitalist society takes to itself the function of justice, on behalf of the people. But it does not *act* on behalf of the people, it acts with its own vested interests, while maintaining the fiction that this is the collective will of the people. The State takes to itself the functions of the investigation of crime and the administration of the juridical structure.

In the particular case of Steven Shaw, almost everything which could humanly be done in terms of campaigning, investigating and legal prosecution has been done, or is being done. Yet the results appear to be lamentable; they clearly highlight the lack of possibilities open to public parties in any battle with the police. To assume, however, either that these efforts were a waste of time, or alternatively that any simple change in the accountability of the police would solve the present impasse and hand back to the people power over justice, is clearly wrong. We are dealing here not simply with formal mechanisms but with consciousness and political processes. The political consciousness of the police will not change in response to structural, legal or juridical reforms of the kind presently being discussed by the Labour Party. Nor will it change by the induction of more black or women officers; the police consciousness is stronger than either sex role orientation or ethnicity. Consciousness is based institutionally upon the relationship of the individual and the institution to personal and political power, the State, and the means of production, exchange and consumption.

Throughout the campaign and the investigation of both the Leon Brittan visit and the subsequent harassment, Manchester City Council responded, corporately and individually, with an exemplary political intelligence and courage. They did not once renege on their responsibilities and they were always ready to provide the necessary resources and time. Politically they kept strictly and with principle to the matter in hand; crime within the Greater Manchester Police force. Unfortunately they were doing this at a time when they were under increasing attack not only from central government but also from the Parliamentary Labour Party, for their policies on policing. Gerald Kaufman, literally the *shadow* Home Secretary, and coincidentally a Manchester M.P., not content with public silence over the campaign of harassment, chose a fringe meeting at the Police Federation conference in 1986, to curry favour with the police and abuse the policing policies of Manchester City Council [89].

In doing this, Kaufman exposed both himself and the Parliamentary Labour Party as condoning State terror and police repression. He publically negated the experience of violence and intimidation to which socialists *and others* in Manchester were desperately trying to give plausibility. Kaufman's aquiescence on the one hand, and public criticism *in front of the police*, of Manchester City Council on the other, shows the policies of the Parliamentary Labour Party to be dictated not by an empathy with the victim, or the possible power of the employed and unemployed 'working class,' but by a fear of the power of its enemies. Policies of collaboration on this level are policies of cowardice.

The discourse about accountability is however important and must be understood within a complex of future socialist policies. Without a policy on criminal justice, the policing function, and prison sentencing policy, the ideological direction of socialism is inevitably utopian. Struggling within a sea of reaction, many socialists tend to forget however, when it comes to matters of law, the first principle of insurgency; *to build institutions and organs within the insurgent class and the community generally which can pursue new and morally different objectives from those of the ruling power*. The present policies on accountability espoused by the Parliamentary Labour Party do not approach this scenario.[90] What is more, when city council politicians in Manchester tried to build these kinds of organisations in the Steven Shaw case, the Parliamentary Labour Party ran for the cover of State institutions. Labour Party plans for accountability are only structural reforms at State level. They reach little further than financial and administrative intereference with local parts of the policing function and have nothing to do with power over the police.

Accountability is about power and about returning the control over investigation and the juridical system to the people. In order to examine the necessary changes in the present structure of accountability which would be consistent with giving the victims of state injustice a voice, we can examine the Manchester case and try to see what mechanisms might have given Steven Shaw and Sarah Hollis access to immediate legal justice.

Accountability: The Criminal Police

The harassment of Steven Shaw and other students following the visit of Leon Brittan could be seen as a clearly articulated *unofficial* response from Greater Manchester police officers to the city administration's call for greater accountability. As the calls for accountability become louder and are illustrated by public inquiries and research into the police, the police build their own defences. At the top, the Chief Constable rails against remaining democratic constraints on his power; at the bottom, uniformed officers seek refuge in anonymity by obscuring their collar numbers, and other officers forsake their uniforms to become, for the time of their criminality at least, unrecognised civilians.

If ever a case showed the illusory nature of the present call for accountability, it was the Steven Shaw case. If ever a case showed how separately powerful and politically conscious the police now are, it is this case. Administrative and financial structures of accountability alone can not cut through the sinister cultural hegemony created by the police. The Avon and Somerset investigation threw up more questions of accountability than it answered. Let us examine some of the 'built-in' anomalies in the present system.

Police officers who might have committed offences on the steps of Manchester University students union were never interviewed but simply asked to write their own statements on interview schedules. (Perhaps the police would be willing to introduce this system for all suspects!) The reasons for this are clear; the police reserve for themselves the full portion of rights and liberties theoretically afforded by bourgeois law at its most progressive. They can not be interviewed about possible crimes without having a solicitor with them, and without 'reasonable suspicion.'

Meanwhile, the victims of assault themselves, tracked to ground and interviewed by police officers regardless of whether they wished to be, gave lengthy statements under conditions which, in some cases, resembled interrogation. Statements were taken without solicitors present and without the complainant knowing the full ambit of the inquiry, or if their statements might be used to help prosecute other students. Few, if any, complainants were given copies of their statements. No complainants have been informed about how their complaints have proceeded.

Even at the end of the Avon and Somerset Inquiry, the police alone were the only body in full knowledge of the planning and the policy behind the police operation on March 1st. The police force is an excessively secret and closed institution. Their attitude to secrecy is pathological and is not commensurate with any form of democracy. This secrecy makes it impossible for anyone other than the police to conduct an investigation into their actions. Complainants, upon whose behalf the State might later decide to prosecute, were never shown photographs with names and numbers of officers involved but were,as is always the case, left to muster what small quantity of facts they could with the help of private but sympathetic parties and no practical help from the investigating officers. Internal police complaints investigations do not even come close to providing the complainant with the tools, to which he or she is entitled under the most minimal requirements of natural justice, one of which must be access to information.

Avon and Somerset officers, who were the only people privy to information from senior officers within the Greater Manchester force, were allowed to form their own picture and work upon their own subjective assumptions in relation to the events which led up to the assaults. There was no democratic guiding constraint imposed on their prejudices. Because there was no objective outside agency present while they conducted their investigation, they were able simply to consider the facts which fitted their own assumptions.

Steven Shaw's case in particular threw up blinding anomalies in the investigative function undertaken by Avon and Somerset officers. Although the Police Complaints Authority handed over the criminal investigation into Steve's custody in Bootle Street to Avon and Somerset officers, these officers acted with incredulity and disbelief when interviewing both witnesses and victim. While they appeared to be carrying out their inquiry into the events on March 1st. with some semblance of efficiency, when it came to the harassment and attacks, they threw all normal policing rules and practices out of the window and adopted an attitude of extreme prejudice to the victims.

The personal and professional dilemma for investigating officers was fundamental. If they began a serious investigation of the assaults, accepting that they came within the ambit of the Police Complaints Authority,then an admission was implied that these offences were committed by police officers. If however the investigating officers determined by reason of their own subjective consciousness that police officers *were not* involved, who then was to investigate these serious criminal attacks? The victims were left in the dark and the criminal investigation in abeyance because the Avon and Somerset officers were unable personally, to accept that police officers might have committed the crimes. In effect, what happened was that the investigating officers fell between two stools; on the one hand accepting a brief from the Police Complaints Authority on behalf of Steven Shaw and against unamed officers from the Greater Manchester Police while on the other hand they spent their investigation attempting to disprove that police officers were involved. Vested interests in this case, not only allowed police officers to go scott free, but also jeopardised the lives of two young students.

If the State investigates, then the State also prosecutes; in England there is not, in any sense of the expression a peoples' prosecution service. If the Avon and Somerset detectives discovered crimes of assault, grievious bodily harm or actual bodily harm committed against students, why did this evidence have to go to another State functionary, the Director of Public Prosecutions. Any evidence of this kind should have been given directly to the complainant's solicitor. If the D.P.P then made a political decision which was not to the liking of the complainant, the complainant would be able to take a private prosecution against those uncovered by the police investigation. The position now, even with new rulings on disclosure, is that Steve Shaw will probably have to take a legal action against the State before his solicitor even has access to results of an investigation apparently begun on his behalf. The fact that there is no people's prosecution service throws up a number of anomalies in a case like that of Steven Shaw, these deserve serious consideration.

In cases where it is suspected that the police have committed crimes against citizens, but where no one has been charged, and where it is evident the the police have failed to fulfill their duties as investigators, what facility is there for legal aid to investigate the case? Why is it that in England, as against the United States, the legal profession is, on the whole, so uncommitted to the rights of individual citizens, that they have not seen to it that there are precedents for suing the police for negligence and failure to fulfill their professional duties?

What facilities are there for disclosure of documents in cases where no legal action has yet been taken against the police? Do the police investigate cases on behalf of victims or are they a power to themselves investigating on behalf of the State? Why is there no facility by which a complainant or their solicitor might have immediate access to all documents upon which a particular police operation has been ordered, or of an investigation which is apparently carried out on their behalf?

If an individual has had a crime committed against him or her by police officers, to which State agency, other than the police, might they turn in order to begin a private investigation?

How is it possible for an 'independent' police investigation to obtain voluntary statements specifically for that investigation but then hand them over to the prosecuting authorities, to be used against witnesses or their friends? Although it is possible in English law for the police to obtain their evidence in any manner they wish, even using tricks and deception, the fact that this appeared to be done by Avon and Somerset officers shows clearly that they were aligning themselves with the State as a prosecutor, rather than with those who were complaining against the State's agents.

The police surgeon who first examined Steven Shaw after he had been assaulted in February was contractually obliged to the Greater Manchester Police, not the P.C.A., or Steven Shaw as a private party. The documentation of Steven's injuries, important evidence, and helpful to him in prosecuting police officers, went directly to Deputy Chief Constable John Stalker. Once again, we can see how the State denies the individual information which might help them prosecute or take action against the State. Where does this place the police surgeon, surely he should have been responsible to Steve Shaw and not the State, to his ethics as a doctor not to the police?

Every witness who might have been instrumental in gaining a conviction for conspiracy to burgle, assault, or perverting the course of justice, against Greater Manchester police officers was interviewed first by Avon and Somerset officers. The issue here is not simply that the police are investigating themselves but that the legal representatives of Steven Shaw and Sarah Hollis were not present at these interviews, nor were they sent the papers. Even more serious, the content of these statements appear have been communicated in one form or another to the GMP and a number of witnesses have since received threats.

It becomes quite clear when examining the history of the Avon and Somerset investigation, and the 'built in' anomalies, that the prefix of 'independent' cannot be seriously attached to the Police Complaints Authority. The conclusion has to be drawn that the State can not investigate and prosecute its own agents or agencies.

Accountability: A Crisis of Faith

There is a fundamental conflict of analysis which determines contemporary position on accountability. The conflict grows out of different definitions of the role of the State in post-industrial society. Those who believe that it is still possible for the policing function to be a localised municipal service also believe that the internal contradiction within the State can be exploited and utilised in the employment of an efficient local force answerable to the lower tiers of the executive administration: the county, the city or the local authority.

Those on the other hand, who believe that the State has a hegemony and a leading ideological function which is a guiding principle of power over the 'working class,' believe that the economic and civil administration inevitably becomes more centralised and that the policing function responds in time only to this central political will. These people tend to believe as well, that the lower tiers of the executive are quickly becoming a reflection of the central State. They believe that rather than being resolved in favour of liberal ideology, the internal contradictions within the State at the moment are more liable to be resolved by the power of the police over the political representatives of capital. The resolution of this contradiction in favour of the police would take us from an authoritarian regime to a police state. The police finally become the 'executive' and they perform the function of civil administration solely to order and control the population. This high degree of control is necessary for capital to make a transition to a society based entirely upon a high technology means of production.

What many analysts of both camps fail to explore, is the structure of accountability that did exist until recently, and what this signified in practice for control over the police by the people as a whole or their democratically elected representatives. What is it that has led to accountability suddenly becoming such an issue for the Labour Party? Which side of the accountability partnership is it, that has disrupted the cosy existence shared by the police force *with all political parties* since their inception in 1829. It is the police who have wriggled out from under even this lightweight counterpane of constraint.

The State in the form of the Home Office, first opened the division between locally elected politicians and the police when they gained a stake within the constabulary Police Authorities in the 1964 Police Act. The police were quick to exploit the new tripartite agreement by siding with the State and suddenly claiming that their new masters had always been their masters, that in fact,they had never had any responsibility to elected politicians. What has increased this apparent separation between the State and the police on the one hand, and the local politicians on the other, is the continued and increasing politicisation of the police in conjunction with the new power which their relationship with the central State administration has given them.

What has occurred in the last few years is a crisis of faith between a crudely politicised police force, on a national level, and that part of the executive which works towards a socialist administration. This crisis of faith is reflected, though less noticeably, even in the relationship between local politicians from the Conservative Party and the Liberal Party and the Police. The new crisis of faith is manifest in reality by a falling out between one element of the middle class and another; the police and local politicians of all hues, but especially and symbolically Labour Party representatives.

It is important to understand who is in the forefront of this schism, which element is breaking away from which other element. While the Labour Party has changed little, the police have changed enormously, and it is always they who are calling the tune and doing the breaking away. As the Parliamentary Labour Party runs after them, trying to make up the argument, it begins to redefine its legal policies to accommodate the police.

Viewed from this perspective, the call for accountability is a cry for *acceptability* from the Labour Party to the police. It is the manifestation of an internal conflict within the ruling groups themselves and is only marginally related to pressure from, or any adverse effects upon, the 'working class'. The Parliamentry Labour Party actually recognises the will to power of the police force and their attempt to share power within the executive; it is now trying to accommodate this.

Calls for accountability by the Parliamentary Labour Party are simply attempts to placate and reassure elements within the working class, the marginalised and the radical populations—their historical constituency—while in reality they are organising to act *with* and on behalf of the police themselves.

What the Manchester case illustrates is that a politically conscious police force now inhabits a new realm of State power. This new realm of power is accommodated and silently acquiesced in by Labour Party politicians because they do not want to appear to be critical of the police at this point in time. In Manchester, a large group of police officers are able to organise a complex form of political social control over a number of people. They can do this without fear of criticism, either from other police officers or from any element within the judiciary. They appear to do it with complete confidence because their actions are tacitly condoned by both the major political parties. Just as the public order policing of March 1st, was an introduction to a new style of policing democratic dissent, so its aftermath has been an introduction to a new form of political control which with the continued acquiescence of both the major parties will, in the future, become the norm.

Having moved in recent years from their control and usurpation of the juridical realm, into the civil administration, the police are now moving into the community to mediate political dissent by taking coercive action against symbolic and actual politically active individuals. That role, which used to be reserved for the Special Branch, is now assumed by large numbers of uniformed and plain clothes officers.

All modes of political representatives need organisation. It is clear that within the Greater Manchester Police Force, that organisation is functioning. It can and will operate against anyone who publically expresses an alternative reality to that articulated by the police. A programme of accountability cannot even be considered until that particularly corrupt organisation is broken up. It cannot be broken up without a democratic and open debate between politicians and police officers in Manchester, linked with a very exacting and fairly intrusive control exerted on the Greater Manchester force by people completely independent of it.

Accountability: The Peoples Tribunal

We have learnt an enormous amount from the case of Steven Shaw and the demonstration on the steps of Manchester University Student Union. One lesson is central; as long as we share our reality with the police and allow them to inhabit it, they will distort it and we will become the victims of our own belief in that illusion which they present to the world. Never trust the police. Their aims and objectives are determined by the State and the separation which has grown between the State and the people means inevitably that they can never act on our behalf, however intelligent or benign they might be as individuals.

The people are bereft of protection because their very identity is a threat to the State. Inevitably, other groups found this out long before white middle class students were forced to these conclusions. Those whose identity has always been a threat to the social relations which make up the State; the unionised working class, the unorganised and criminal working class, the Irish, the black and women in certain spheres, have known for years that their identity and form of social relations was a threat to the British capitalist State.

The only way to combat the pervasive reality of a police defined society is for those who are in opposition to build their own reality; to form their own autonomous political and civil structures. This cannot be done in relation to the police alone but has to be done in every sphere of life.

With respect to the police, the first task is to understand and know as much about them as they understand and know about us. Research is vital, not simply abstract or academic research but real information about their organisation and culture. This research and information has to be used politically, it has to be presented in ways which the working class and the marginalised can understand. It has to bear a relationship to the everyday lives of those who know intuitively that the police are actually controlling agents of the State.

The conflict between the State and the people leaves a vaccuum of protection. As the State draws into itself and the sole purpose of its agencies becomes the defence of a small elite, the great mass of the people are left to survive by their own resources. All institutions of care and protection are withdrawn from those who have become not only enemies of the State but also worthless to the productive system. The people have to organise their own institutions and organs of protection and welfare; this is just as true of policing agencies and self defence groups as it is of health centres.

One of the most important lessons we are learning during Steven's case is how to defend and protect an individual like Steven. However, we should not have had to struggle with this; the organisations, the community, the networks should have been built by now as they have been in refuges for female victims of male violence and by black groups for victims of racial attack. These structures have not been built for the left and victims of State violence.

The growing separation between the State and the people leaves us not only to defend ourselves but also to seek out and investigate those who commit offences against us. In this, there are no short cuts. The minute and detailed work of investigation has to be done, piecing together a reality which coincides with the facts, the evidence and the proof. We need not worry that we can not do this as well as the police, they in fact have grown fat and lazy, they are on the whole inefficient investigators. They demur from proper scientific investigation and indulge in ideologically based speculation to resolve the intricate social problems with which they are faced. We can enquire into crimes committed against us, with a greater understanding of the community we live within, and using a more sympathetic social philosophy.

As each incident happened to Steven Shaw, it should have been throughly investigated. Photographs should have been taken; witnesses sought out; statements taken. Information should have been correlated, giving leads on possible sources of the harassment and motivation for it. In the first instance, the demonstration on the steps should not have taken place without people being properly organised to take notes and photographs, make tapes, record video film and without individuals who made it their task to take the numbers of all vans and cars at the scene. Nothing can now be taken for granted between the people and the police, we have to move onto another footing.

While investigations can be done, the question of justice is more complex. There are no peoples' courts, we do not even have anything resembling the 'red' judges or magistrates of Italy. In the community and in the workplace, the age old censure can be enacted on many levels, from 'sending to Coventry' through to banishment or expulsion from the community, as has always been done within the working class in the case of informers and agents. There have so far been no sanctions used against the Greater Manchester Police by either the City Council or the University administration over the attacks on Steve or Sarah. Both these institutions should declare moratoriums on any contact between themselves and the police until someone in the GMP takes public responsibility for what has happened. It is necessary for both these organisations to show the public condemnation of all Manchester citizens to the behaviour of the Greater Manchester Police.

In cases which involve crimes against the people by the State, we have only limited ways of presenting our evidence to the public; public tribunals and reports are two of them. The independent and public Inquiry set up by Manchester City Council, and its consequent report, was a major step forward in this respect. Such inquiries and reports, and the basic concept of the public tribunal which they entail, should be ongoing and frequent with respect to the police. For too long now we have been the victims of the State's reality, we have to begin presenting our own.

If the presentation of our investigations entials the naming of guilty parties, even if we know that State courts will not come to the same conclusions, we should make these names public. Although certain individuals within the media are to be trusted, the corporate control of all media and therefore much of the representation of our reality, is in the hands of the State. We have to develop our own means of representation and we have to make public our inquiries, our tribunals and our investigations, through our own media.

The individual in a post industrial society cannot take on the State alone. However much popular bourgois culture tries to seduce us with the lone and romantic male investigator whether State employed or private, his hour is passed. Only the organised strength of the people can take on the State, and within that force we will have to begin developing all the functions which keep alive the organism of a complex society.

CHRONOLOGY

1984	Michael Heseltine daubed with red paint on a visit to Manchester University Students' Union.
13.2.85	Leon Brittan visits Queen Mary College, London; enters by back door rather than face a picket at the front.
	John Carlisle prevented by demonstration from speaking at Bradford University on "Sport and South Africa."
	Trial of Jackie Berkeley begins in Manchester.
Mid-Feb 85	Michael Heseltine pelted with eggs at Glasgow University; advised by police not to speak at Strathclyde.
16.2.85	Michael Fallon MP attacked at Sunderland Polytechnic.
17.2.85	John Carlisle prevented from speaking at Oxford University by an occupation of the meeting room. Advised by police to "get out of town".
19.2.85	Planned visit of John Carlisle to Leeds Polytechnic cancelled following incidents at Bradford and Oxford.
25.2.85	First of a series of weekly demonstrations against Professor John Vincent at Bristol University in response to his column in "The Sun".
1.3.85	**Leon Brittan visits Manchester Students' Union.**
2.3.85	Press coverage of demonstration: *Daily Mail:*

	''Police Aid Brittan Demo Girl''
	Manchester Evening News:
	''Police stormed Manchester University Students' Union....Police presence was massive....It was was clear that they were not going to allow a repeat of last year's violence....(against) Michael Heseltine.'' Final edition carries photographs of arrests and of Sarah Hollis injured on the steps of the Union.
	Daily Mirror:
	''Police 'Put Boot In' ....Students' Union General Secretary quoted as saying, 'There were some very ugly scenes of police violence and brutality.'''
	Daily Express:
	''a number of women students were punched and kicked in a police charge.''
	Guardian
	''100 policemen arrived....scuffles broke out.''
	Daily Telegraph:
	''a huge police presence....in ugly scenes resembling those on miners' picket lines about 100 uniformed police cleared steps.''
4.3.85	Steven Shaw meets Steven Wright at the Police Monitoring Unit.
	Defendants' meeting at the Union followed by meeting at the Town Hall between Students Union representatives and staff of Police Monitoring Unit.
5.3.85	Steven Shaw finds door to flat at Top of the Meadow Farm broken and thesis missing.
	Emergency meeting of Students' Union adopts policy of non-cooperation with police complaints procedure. Meeting of defence campaign for those arrested.
6.3.85	Steven Shaw stopped for a traffic violation on the Stockport Road.
10.3.85	Following a meeting of the Greater Manchester Police Authority, *Manchester Evening News* reports Anderton's irritation over the Authority's call for a public inquiry into the policing of the

demonstration.

11.3.85 John Reddington, Deputy Chief Constble of Avon and Somerset, arrives in Manchester to conduct police inquiry into events of March 1st.

15.3.85 First Court appearances for those arrested on 1st March. Magistrates reject defence lawyers' application for a joint defence.

21.3.85 University Senate passes resolution affirming right to free speech and to peaceful assembly and demonstration. Resolution also expressed grave concern at reports of police behaviour and calls for official independent inquiry.

22.3.85 Leon Brittan, speaking on a visit to the Equal Opportunity Commission in Manchester, rejects possibility of a public inquiry and says that it was his decision to use the front door rather than enter by the back. (He repeats this in a letter to Alf Morris MP).

25.3.85 Manchester AUT (Association of University Teachers) writes to Manchester Central MP, Bob Litherland, calling for a public inquiry into the policing of the demonstration.

Steven Shaw leaves Manchester for London to stay with his family.

NUS President Phil Woolas, opening the Union's Easter Conference, launches a bitter attack on the government for trying to discredit NUS: "...those in and out of parliament who want the NUS declared illegal....Ministers provoke and treat free speech like a political football."

End of March Avon and Somerset inquiry begins its investigations

9.4.85 Trials of those arrested begin: hearings continue almost without interruption throughout April and May.

23.4.85 Dom Wall notices for the first time that his flat is under surveillance.

25.4.85 Steven Shaw returns to Top of the Meadow Farm and begins rewriting his thesis.

29.4.85	Charles Alcock's case begins and Sarah Hollis attends as a witness. Alcock is acquited. Sarah Hollis followed from the court by a police van. New Police Complaints Authority comes into existence.
2.5.85	Sarah Hollis followed by white police van as she cycles from her home to the University.
3.5.85	Sarah Hollis followed from her home to the University by police van again. Police Complaints Authority issue statement that they will be taking over supervision of the Avon and Somerset investigation.
9.5.85	At 3.00.am. Sarah Hollis receives first of a series of anonymous phone calls. Dom Wall followed by red Cortina. Steven Shaw stopped in Rusholme on another traffic violation.
10.5.85	Sarah Hollis gets another anonymous phone call. Steven Shaw speaks in Students' Union meeting against cooperation with Avon and Somerset inquiry. He then returns to London to collect retyped thesis.
11.5.85	Sarah Hollis stopped by uniformed motorcycle police while riding her bicycle on Oxford Road. Asked for her name and address and questioned about her movements.
13.5.85	Sarah Hollis's flat burgled in the early hours of the morning. Later she receives two more anonymous phone calls. Steven Shaw returns to Manchester.
14.5.85	Steven Shaw stopped by plain clothes police officer and taken to Bootle Street police station, where he is held for five hours and assaulted.
15.5.85	Sarah Hollis meets Reddington and other officers from Avon and Somerset. She makes a statement about the events of March 1st and states her intention of making a formal complaint against the

officers who threw her down the steps. She also mentions subsequent harassment. Later that day she is threatened by two men in a car while cycling home from the Students' Union.

Following the events of the previous few days both Steven Shaw and Sarah Hollis go into hiding, only returning to Manchester in late May/early June in order to take their examinations.

20.5.85	Steven Shaw stopped for yet another traffic violation. Later he travels to London to revise.
22.5.85	Independent Inquiry Panel appointed by Manchester City Council to investigate the policing of the Brittan demonstration and subsequent events. To be chaired by John Platt-Mills, Q.C.
24.5.85	Sarah Hollis receives an anonymous phone call.
25.5.85	Sarah Hollis receives another anonymous phone call. Jackie Berkeley found guilty of 'wasting police time'.
End of May	Witness statements taken by Avon and Somerset investigators in connection with the policing of the demonstration are handed over to Greater Manchester Police prosecutors. Defence solicitors meet John Reddington to protest.
5.6.85	Steven Shaw returns to Manchester and sits first finals paper. Independent Inquiry panel writes to James Anderton inviting his cooperation.
7.6.85	Anderton writes to independent Inquiry panel declining invitation for his officers to submit evidence. Steven Shaw approached outside Whitworth Park by a police officer who verbally notes his new address. From this point until the end of his exam on June 20th he is under frequent surveillance from police vehicles parked near the accommodation.

11.6.85	Sarah Hollis followed on and off three buses.
13.6.85	White police van parked outside Sarah Hollis' new address, which she has tried to keep secret.
15.6.85	Independent Inquiry holds first public hearing in Manchester Town Hall.
	Sarah Hollis gives evidence in camera.
	Later she is followed by two men in a red car who threatened her with rape and further hospitalisation.
16.6.85	Second day of public hearings.
17.6.85	Amanda Hughes and Frank Logan arrested for burglary of Sarah Hollis's flat.
20.6.85	Steven Shaw finishes last exam and returns to London.
25.6.85	GLC Police Monitoring Committee Support Unit burgled.
26.6.85	Manchester Police Monitoring Unit broken into.
27.6.85	Steven Shaw gives evidence to independent inquiry panel in London.
12.7.85	Manchester City Council Police Monitoring Unit suggest that M15 or Special Branch may have been responsible fo the break in at their offices.
19.7.85	Home of Police Monitoring Unit worker Ann Lewis broken into.
22.7.85	John Stalker refers Bootle Street incident to Avon and Somerset inquiry.
	Guardian and *Manchester Evening News* report the harassment of the two students.
7.8.85	Avon and Somerset investigators start making enquiries about Steven Shaw through the University, asking for a copy of his thesis.
28.9.85	Reddington replaced as head of police investigation by Alan Vickers, Deputy Chief Constable of South Wales.
11.10.85	Cases of seven of those convicted following demonstration go to Appeal Court. Three appeals upheld, four dismissed.
31.10.85	Report of independent inquiry published. BBC 'Brass Tracks' programme covers policing of

	demonstration.
Early Nov:	Avon and Somerset investigators contact Steven Shaw's London solicitors.
November:	David Hunt MP, Minister for Coal, demonstrated against at Nottingham University.
9.11.85	David Waddington visits Manchester University. Attacked by students angered by speech on immigration made two weeks previously.
13.11.85	University Council issues Students' Union with a deadline of November 26th to produce the names of the students involved in Waddington incident.
15.11.85	Sarah Hollis followed around central Manchester by two men, one of whom she recognises from an earlier encounter. She is threatened, jostled and physically assaulted. Union agrees to produce a report on the Waddington incident, but without naming names. Report accuses Waddington of incitement.
20.11.85	BBC 'Out of Court' programme covers the policing of the demonstration and subsequent events. A letter from John Stalker to the programme rejects the findings of the independent inquiry and cites the attack on Waddington in support of his view that a core of violent students exists in the Manchester University campus.
27.11.85	University Council finds report inadequate and appoints disciplinary committee. Four students suspended (tantamount to explusion).
15.1.85	Sarah Hollis watched by two men, one of whom she recognises, as she leaves a friend's house in Rusholme.
17.1.86	Sarah Hollis followed by marked police car as she cycles to Monsall Hospital.
22.1.86	Steven Shaw interviewed by Avon and Somerset officers at his solicitor's office in London. Interview lasts seventeen hours, fifty-eight page statement produced.
24.1.86	Manchester University buildings occupied in sup-

	port of suspended students. University Council granted eviction order by High Court.
28.1.86	Sarah Hollis attacked outside Ducie High School on Upper Lloyd Street.
30.1.86	Steven Shaw goes to Manchester by train; arrives late afternoon and notices a number of uniformed officers standing near ticket barrier.
2.2.86	Steven Shaw, alone in friends' house, goes out to get tobacco and is attacked by two men.
4.2.86	Sarah Hollis leaves Manchester for safety. Steven Shaw transferred to a hospital in London.
10.2.86	Second occupation of University, involving 100 students. University Authorities order repossession of buildings with Court order issued in January.
11.2.86	First reading of Private Member's Bill by Fred Sylvester, MP for Withington (Manchester), to "safeguard the right of Free Speech in Universities and Institutions of Higher Education." Heseltine's and Brittan's visits to Manchester cited in introductory speech.
21.2.86	Suspended students lodge an appeal.
5.3.86	Demonstration against George Walden, Parliamentary Under Secretary of State, at Bolton Institute of Higher Education.
Week of 10.3.86	Sarah Hollis withdraws complaint against the police.
14.3.86	Second reading of Sylvester Bill, introduced and read by John Carlisle, supported by George Walden.
17.3.86	Keith Joseph, Minister for Education, pelted with eggs etc. by 500 demonstrators at University College, Swansea.
24.3.86	Full page *Guardian* article. Press Conference at the House of Commons on Steve's case.
27.3.86	Manchester City Council requests interview with Home secretary Douglas Hurd to discuss the delay in the Avon and Somerset Inquiry.

1.4.86 Manchester University Senate passes resolution calling for a judicial inquiry into the attacks on Steven Shaw and Sarah Hollis in the event of no action being taken against GMP officers by the beginning of the 1986/87 academic year.

6.6.86 Avon and Somerset Report sent to the Director of Public Prosecutions.

References and Notes

Preface

1 Some revealing examples of police assumptions are given in the field training manual for police officers written by the ex-Deputy Assistant Commissioner of the Metropolitan Police, David Powis. Amongst those likely to be involved in crime he mentions: women without handbags, male joggers wearing track suits (possible 'homosexual nuisance'), young men driving new cars, men with dirty hands ('an honest mechanic, so often a family man, will purchase and use chemical cleaners for he has to be clean at family meals'), and people who carry 'these are your rights' cards! See *The Signs of Crime: Field Manual for Police,* McGraw Hill, 1977.

Introduction

2 The Director of Public Prosecutions is the legal adviser to the State; he is answerable to the Attorney General who is a political appointee of the incumbent executive. The approval of the DPP must be sought before certain proceedings can be instituted (See also note 4).

3 In summing up in rape cases Judges are advised to warn the Jury about convicting if corroborative forensic evidence is absent. *Archbold* (1985) says: "The jury should be warned in plain language that it is dangerous to convict on the evidence of the complainant, because experience has shown that female complainants have told false stories....On a charge of rape the corroborative evidence must confirm in some material particular that intercourse has taken place without the woman's consent, and also that the defendant was the man who committed the crime."

4 Section 5 of the Criminal Law Act 1967, part 2, states that; "Where a person causes any wasteful employment of the police by knowingly making to any person a false report tending to show than an offence has been committed, or to give rise to apprehension for the safety of any person or property, or tending to show that he has information material to any police inquiry, he shall be liable on summary conviction to imprisonment for not more than six months or to a fine of not more than level 4 on the standard scale." The law also makes it clear that no proceedings can be instituted under this section without the approval of the Director of Public Prosecutions.

5 "The Creed of a Devout Copper," interview with James Anderton by John Mortimer, *Sunday Times Magazine,* 2nd November 1980.

6 Lord Hewlett Memorial Lecture by James Anderton, reported in the *Manchester Evening News,* 16th March 1982.

7 Manchester police were publicly issued with Heckler and Koch machine guns at Manchester airport on January 9th 1986. However, Metropolitan police officers have carried sub-machine guns on anti-terrorist and diplomatic duties at various times in the past.

8 The County Police Authorities were broken up when the Metropolitan County Councils were disbanded on 1st April 1986. The bodies which replaced them are also called Police Authorities but are sometimes referred to as Joint Boards to distinguish them from their predecessors. The old Police Authority was made up of directly elected county councillors whereas the Joint Board comprises councillors nominated by district councils (ten in the case of Greater Manchester), with a third of the board being made up of local magistrates.

9 *Police Review,* 29the March 1985, reported Anderton as saying in a local radio interview, ''It does appear to the public that the police have imposed a kind of curfew on the community as a whole, not just the miners, and also that they have restricted free movement. These features are things we normally only associate with countries behind the iron curtain.''

10 Ibid. 6.

11 BBC Question Time, October 16th 1979.

12 ''Constabularly duty should be left as it is,'' article by James Anderton in *The Guardian,* March 29th 1985.

13 Ibid. 6. Implicit in this statement and that of many other senior police officers is the idea that they alone can diagnose ''the common good.''

14 Ibid. 6.

15 AGM of the Greater Manchester Police Federation, reported in *Police Review,* November 15th 1985.

16 ''Housing and the Inner City Crisis—A Police Review,'' institute of Housing Annual Conference, Harrogate, June 18th 1984.

17 Harold Salsbury, ex-Chief Constable of South Yorkshire, interviewed on BBC Panorama, 2nd March 1981:
Interviewer: ''Which groups are in your files here?''
Salsbury: ''Oh, anyone who shows any affinity towards communism, that's common sense! The IRA, the PLO and I would say anyone who's decrying marriage and family life, trying to break that up; pushing drugs or advocating the acceptance of certain drugs, homosexuality, indiscipline in schools, weak

penalties for anti-social crimes, pushing that sort of thing. A whole gamut of things like that, which could be pecking away at the foundations of society and weakening it.''
Interviewer: ''Do you regard such people as subversive?''
Salsbury: ''In a word, yes.''
James Anderton has also described those worthy of policy attention as 'social nonconformists, malingerers, idlers, parasites, spongers, frauds, cheats and unrepentant criminals.' (quoted in *The Powers of Policing* by Martin Kettle.)

18 Ibid. 5.

19 James Anderton, ''How on earth do they expect us to cope?'', *Police Review*, 15th November 1985.

Chapter 1 — Waiting for Leon

20 During the miners' strike, Manchester Polytechnic Students' Union loaned Bold NUM several thousand pounds. Bold were later unable to repay the money, giving rise to intense police investigation into the Student's Union accounts. According to existing regulations a student union can not donate over £100 to a fund which is not directly associated with their education.

21 The guidelines issued by the Committee of Vice-Chancellors and Principals of the Universities of the United Kingdom were prefaced by a statement from the Chairman. Four general points in this statement make it quite clear that the Committee was unhappy issuing them. Their tone suggests that they did not believe the present government was blameless in the matter.
1. With the decline elsewhere of the open political meeting, universities and other Institutions of higher education find themselves bearing special reponsibility they are in line as a target for small groups of extremists, not always students, who wish to create conflict through provocation.
2. Nothing excuses disruptive or intimidatory behaviour but students must be able to protest and to heckle at meetings as long as lawful freedom of speech and of assembly are not infringed.
3. No university possesses anything remotely like a police force and none would wish to do so.
4. Almost all universities are freely open to access and have no effective way of preventing outsiders from entering their grounds and premises.

22 Sylvester Bill, first reading 11th February 1986.

23 Fred Sylvester MP.

24 See Chronology.

25 The Bill sets out plans for a major rationalisation and restructuring of the whole education system. One of its aims is to end compulsory membership of student unions.

Chapter 2 — Monstrous Regiment

26 This statement and all others quoted in this chapter and chapter 4 were given to the Students' Union following the demonstration.

27 For public order purposes a 'serial' is comprised of 1 inspector, 2 sergeants and 20 constables. Serials are trained in the latest crowd control equipment and manoeuvres and operate as tightly knit units. (From *Riot Training in Greenwich,* a report of the London Borough of Greewich Police Committee Support Unit).

28 All the police officers giving evidence in the court following the demonstration claimed that they were not wearing jewellery or watches due to the risk of damage either to the wearer or to people with whom they came into physical contact.

29 Brittan accused "the stamping and shouting demonstrators of the worst kind of intellectual hypocrisy....They are afraid of hearing the truth." (*Daily Telegraph*, 2nd March 1985). Such phraseology is common amongst Tory MP's and cabinet ministers during their visits to colleges and universities. Six months later David Waddington described demonstrating students on the same campus as "detestable scum that didn't deserve to be at University." (*Daily Mail*, 9 November 1985).

Chapter 3 - Defending the Person of the State

30 See *State of Siege,* Coulter, Miller and Walker, Canary Press, 1984. *State Research Bulletin* (Vol. 2, No. 13), August/September 1979.

31 See "A new look at less lethal weapons." J. Rosenhead, *New Scientist,* December 1976.
The Technology of Political Control, Ackroyd et.al., 1977.
The Policing Revolution, Sarah Mainwaring-White, 1983.
"Plastic Bullets and the Met," in *Policing London,* Greater London Council Police Committee, April/May 1983.
Techno-Cop, Rampet and British Society for Social Responsibility in Science (BSSRS), 1985.
"Hurd backs plastic bullets," *Guardian,* 1st May 1986.
Manual of Tactical Options and Related Matters, internal documents of the Association of Chief Police Officers. (of which only the first nine pages are publicly available.)

32

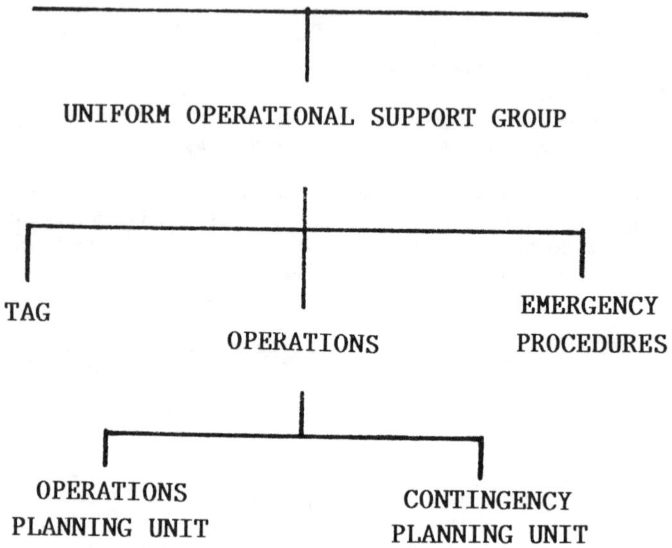

33 *The Fall of Scotland Yard,* Cox, Shirley and Short, Penguin Books, 1977 gives details of widescale corruption and extortion by Metropolitan police officers from the Flying Squad, the Obscene Publications Squad and the Drug Squad.
The Pornbrokers, Martin Tomskin, Virgin Books 1982, further details corruption in the Obscene Publications Squad.
Adams Tale, Honeycombe, Hutchinson 1975, catalogues the extensive practice of police officers accepting bribes.
Further evidence of the corruption of London's Robbery Squad can be found in Nick Davies's report in the *Guardian* on Operation Countryman, 21st July and 3rd August 1982.

34 See "Police Hide Arsenal," A. Jennings and R. Rohrer, *New Statesman,* 13th March 1981.

35 In August 1983 four youths were assaulted on the Holloway Road, North London. They claimed that police officers were responsible. After a successful civil action agains the Metropolitan Police and a two and a half year investigation, the Police Complaints Authority announced that due to lack of evidence no action could be taken against individual police officers. One of the youths, 18 year old Daniel Jenkins, gave evidence detailed enough to identify at least

five of the attackers. Three of the suspects exercised their right to refuse to stand on an identity parade. A concerted public and media campaign forced the Met to reopen the enquiry, under the direction of their head of complaints, David O'Dowd. On Friday 21st 1986 O'Dowd announced that any officer who gave evidence identifying the culprits and who had not himself taken part in the assaults would be given full immunity from prosecution by the DPP. Within twenty four hours four police officers had been charged with conspiracy to commit the assaults on the four boys.

36 See "The Rise of a Tough New Elite", *Sunday Times,* 26th September 1982

37

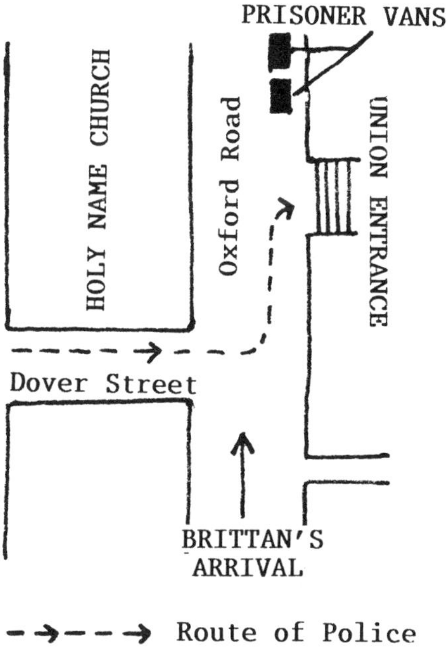

MAP I

38 "Strike Force" by Nick Davies, *Observer Colour Supplement* 1st December 1985 details the Met's martial arts 'arrests and restraint' programme for public order and describes their new chain-stick, officially know as a 'defender-baton.'

39 A 'collar' number is so-called because the older, more traditional police uniform, had a small stand-up collar to which the metal number was attached. Modern uniforms have numbers on the epaulettes. During the miners' strike a large number of officers either blacked out the numbers or didn't wear them at all.

See *Strike Breaking in Essex,* Moira Abdel-Rrahim, Canary Press, 1985 *State of Siege,* Coulter, Miller and Walker, Canary press, 1984, *The State Versus the People; Lesson from the Coal Dispute,* Journal of Law and Society, Vol. 12, No. 3, winter 1985.
At the height of the strike, Tony Benn asked the Home Secretary if officers were supposed to wear their numbers whilst on duty. The answer he received was "no." Following complaints of assaults by unidentifiable officers during the miners strike, the police have said that new uniforms are to have nonremovable numbers (they were formerly attached with velcro). See article in the *Guardian* by Malcolm Dean, 17th August 1986.

40 The initial drafts of the Police and Criminal Evidence Bill contained the much acclaimed safeguard which allowed a suspect to write down the arresting officer's name and number.

41 Ibid. 37

Gutter Culture

42 *Police and People in London,*Smith and Grey, Policy Studies Institute, Gower Publishers, 1985.

43 "A typology of Police Corruption," Roebuck and Barker, *Social Problems* 21:423-37, 1974.
Explaining Crime, New York, Nettler, McGraw Hill, 1974.
The Contrasting Occupation Culture of Policemen and Social Workers; A psychological and sociological review, C.C. Thomas, Springfield, 1973.
Police and People in London (Ibid. 42).

Missing, Presumed Stolen

44 Manchester Police Monitoring Unit was set up by Manchester City Council in February 1985. Currently employing eight full-time workers, the group's main aim is to promote greater police accountability. The unit produces a bi-monthly publication, *Policewatch,* which is delivered free to every house in Manchester.

Chapter 5 — The Trials of Being a Student

45 The legal definition of a 'public place' can be found under section 9 of the 1936 Public Order Act: "Any highway and other premises or place to which at the material time the public have or are permitted to have access." *(Brownlies Law Of Public Order and National Security,* 2nd. edition, 1981 by M. Superstone).

46 Section 5 of the 1936 Public Order Act states that, "Any person who in any public place or public meeting a) uses threatening, abusive or insulting words or behaviour or b) distributes or displays any writing, sign or visible representation which is threatening, abusive and insulting, with intent to provoke a breach of the peace or whereby a breach of the peace is likely to be occasioned, shall be guilty of an offence."

47 See Table of Arrests.

Two Ways of Seeing

48 I want to make the point here that although a relatively large number of uniformed officers were involved in the harassment in an organised manner, none of them committed any physical attacks. We have to conclude from this that some uniformed officers had specific instructions to keep Sarah and Steve under surveillance but neither to arrest nor act violently against them. We can also conclude that this part of the harassment was left to plain clothes officers. How was this agreement between uniformed and plain clothes officers communicated and arranged?

49 'Graft' is corruption and earnings from relationships between police officers, politicians and public servants, out of crime or illegal enterprises, often with criminals; the misuse of authority by a police officers in a manner designed to produce personal gain for himself or others.
See *Police Corruption: A Perspective on its Nature and Control,* Goldstein, Washington Police Foundation, 1975.
"A Theory of Corruption," McMullan, *Sociological Review* No. 9, 1961.
"The Organisation and Social Setting of Police Corruption," Misner, *Police Journal* No. 48, January 1975.

50 A survey of Police Complaints by Ken Russell of Leicester Polytechic covering two police forces showed that approximately half of all complaints were withdrawn, many due to 'fear of reprisals or pressure by investigating officers'. In 1983, of 16,231 complaints filed against police officers, only 10 per cent led to disciplining or 'advising' of an officer, and of 34 charges which it was recommended should be brought, only 6 officers were found guilty. There have been many examples of cases where police have charged complainants with an offence arising out of the incident complained of. (See *The Police Act 1984: A critical guide,* GLC Police Committee Discussion Paper No. 3.

51 DCS Bill Moody was himself later charged with corruption after helping Williamson with the *Times* enquiry. See *The Fall of Scotland Yard,* Ibid. 33.

52 Alan Roberts was charged with the William and Glynn's Bank robbery. He disappeared during the Countryman investigation but his body was never found and non-one was ever charged with his murder. It was generally suspected

that he was about to talk to Countryman officers about police involvement in robberies.

53 See Nick Davies's articles in the *Observer,* Ibid. 33.

Chapter 6 — Fear on the Streets: March

54 See Chronology, March 2nd. 1985 for press coverage. Sarah Hollis made a complaint to the *Daily Mail* about their "Police Help Demo Girl" article but received no reply.

55 An HO/RT1 is a document requesting the driver to produce his or her driving licence, tax, insurance and MOT at a named police station within a period of a week.

Chapter 7 — Fear on the Streets: April

56 The formal mechanism for calling in an outside force to carry out an investigation remains the responsibility of the Assistant Chief Constable, who choses a force of his choice. The only difference since the introduction of the new Police Complaint Authority is that the investigation is now supervised by the PCA. The team from the investigating force must be headed by an Assistant Chief Constable who has not previously been an officer in the force to be investigated.

57 Section 32 of the 1964 Police Act states that "The Secretary of State for the Home Office may cause a local enquiry to be held by a person appointed by him into any matter connected with the policing of any area." The Act gives no indication of the basis on which such a decision would be made.

58 See *Manchester Evening News,* 10th March 1985 for report, 14th March 1985 for letter from Anderton.

59 "Y" Department is a force wide body that deals with all complaints against police officers, internal disciplinary matters and civil claims against the Greater Manchester Police. At the time of writing the Chief Superintendent of the Discipline and Complaints Department is D. Ankers. Mr Ankers was head of CID at Bootle Street in May 1985. In 1985 the department claims to have investigated 1,205 complaints, out of which only 14 officers faced criminal charges.

Chapter 8 — Fear on the Street: May

60 *The Mancunion,* Manchester University Student Union newspaper, 22nd May

1985, reports that detectives from the Avon and Somerset inquiry team had visited students' homes even though they did not wish to cooperate with the inquiry.

61 On 13th March 1985, the Manchester University branch of the AUT unanimously passed the following resolution: "Manchester AUT reaffirms its commitment both to freedom of speech and to the right of lawful assembly and demonstration. It expresses grave concern at reports of police behaviour outside the Students' Union on Friday March 1st, and calls for an official independent inquiry into the tactics and actions of the police on that occasion."

62 On the day following his resignation as the General Secretary of the Student's Union, Craig Russel made a long statement to Avon and Somerset officers.

63 Whilst shopping in the Moss Side Centre, Frank met two officers, both of whom he knew from an incident involving a stolen car. His sworn affidavit, now in the possession of the *Guardian* newspaper, reads as follows: "I greeted them, they started chatting about how I was, whether I had kept out of trouble. I asked them what had happened to the car that they had arrested me in 2-3 yers earlier. I had never been arrested in respect to that car....They asked if I was doing anything at the moment. I understood this to mean whether I was stealing any cars and I gave a non-commital reply. The other officer said to me that if I was going to do anything I should do Sarah Hollis's place. I asked them where she lived. They said she lived at the same Crescent as me, John Nash. I was surprised, I though they were joking. They said something about the flat having a picture of Margaret Thatcher in the window, I still didn't know which flat they were talking about." Later on in the statement Frank claims that when he broke into Sarah's flat he noticed the poster of Margaret Thatcher in the front window.

64 Both Frank Logan and Amanda Hughes were refused bail and spent some time in custody on remand before trial. Neither had an opportunity to speak to the other. When Amanda was released after her trial the first person to contact her was the WPC detective Frank claimed had approached him. We do not know what took place at this meeting. Amanda has told the author that this detective had spoken to her previously in derogatory terms about students in general and Sarah Hollis in particular.

Five Hours in Bootle Street

65 This section is based upon a number of interviews and statements made by Steven Shaw after his custody in Bootle Street. To avoid making the text unnecessarily stilted, I have not detailed the long period of silence which formed a substantial part of the four hours for which Steven was actually sitting in the room with the two men. Bootle Street Police station is the headquarters of 'A' Division.

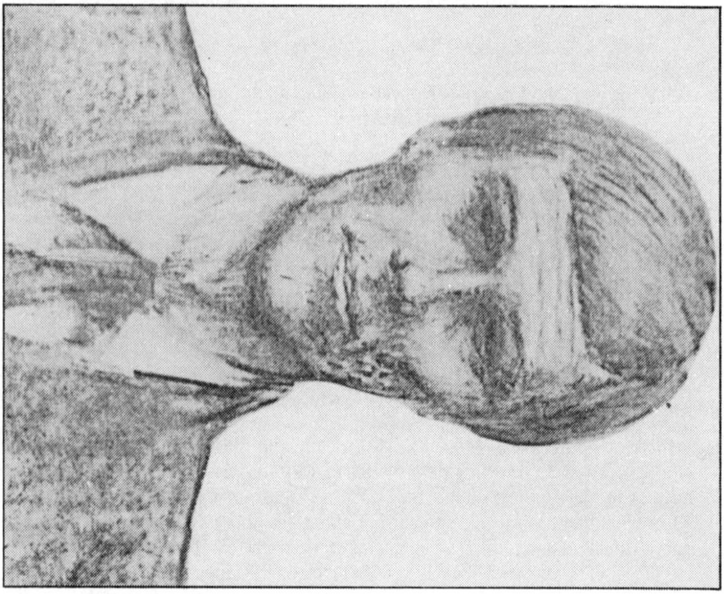

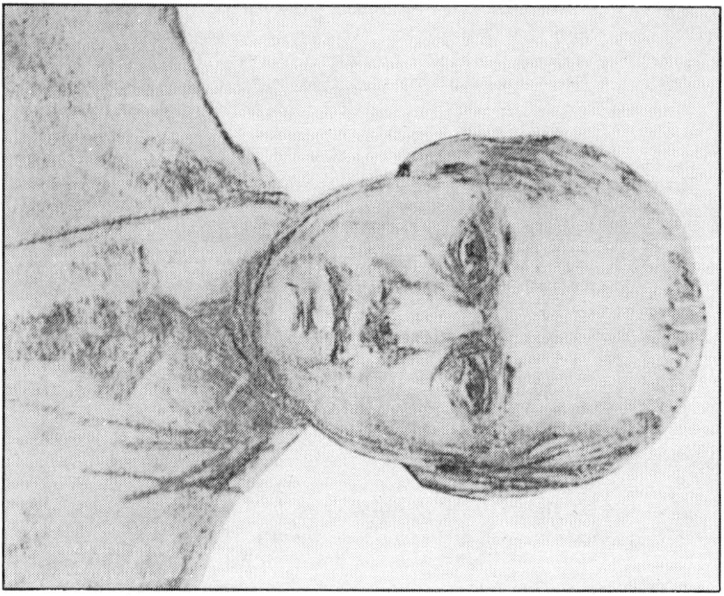

66 The Arwen is a multi-purpose repeater riot gun. Produced at Enfield by the Royal Ordnance Company, it was designed for use by British troops in Ireland. The weapon is capable of firing a combination of baton rounds and CS gas cannisters from its revolving chamber. This weapon has been patented by the British Ministry of Defence in South Africa and appears to have been used during recent rioting in Johannesburg.

67 Bootle Street Police Station has two entrances. One, with a blue lamp over the door, is the entrance through which a member of the public might go into the station. It is also the entrance through which an arrested person would normally be taken. There is a desk sergeant here, and cells for holding prisoners. The remainder of Bottle Street station is entered via a stone arch with tall wire mesh gates and an attendant constable overseeing entering cars. It contains squad and administrative offices. One of the only sections of the station which has unused interview rooms is the Aliens Bureau. This consists of three rooms which might be used only rarely for interviewing people who need to register or who have difficulties with their passports.

68 A full detailed description of the two officers is given in Steve's statement to the Avon and Somerset team on 21st January 1986. "I would described the passenger as late thirties, early forties, 5'11", mousy hair which was greying at the sides and balding. Clean shaven, slightly wrinkled around the top of the cheek bones. No noticeable accent. He was wearing a watch with a black leather strap and gold face.....I recall that the older of the two men has a small pale scar on the inside of his left arm, just below the crook of his arm....I would describe the driver as younger, early thirties, over 6' and athletic looking. Brown hair covering his ears....Local accent. He had acne which appeared worse on the left side of his face." At a much later date Steven's solicitor had artists' impressions of the two men drawn (see facing page). These were published on a 'Wanted' poster by Manchester City Council.

69 According to descriptions given his solicitors it appears most likely that Steve was taken to the Aliens Bureau. The Chief Constable's 1985 Report records that this section is manned by Special Branch officers; "The Branch is responsible for the supervision and registration of aliens and persons entring and leaving this country, and investigations into applications for naturalisation, together with enquiries received from the Home Office."

70 Steve noted this window in his statement to his solicitor soon after the incident, but neglected to mention it in his later statement to the Avon and Somerset officers, Manchester police officers, in private conversations, were later to make much of the fact that no room without a window existed.

71 At times during the period of custody, both men left the room, on one occassion with Steven's clothes. The were obviously at home in the station and were probably mixing with other officers there. The room in which Steve was most probably interviewed is directly across the corridor from the open

plan drugs squad offices.

72 This small white scar was one of the vital distinguishing marks which set this man apart from other officers. Midway through 1986 the Greater Manchester Police made a public statement to the effect that they would examine the arms of officers in Bottle Street police station between the ages of 35 - 45 for this scar. They gave no reassurances that there would be outside observers. Neither did they say whether they would examine the arms of civilian staff. Even this restricted investigation caused the Greater Manchester branch of the Police Federation to issue an immediate statement telling officers that they were not obliged to take part in any examination. Steven Shaw's solicitors were not contacted in relation to this exercise and nothing further was ever heard of the matter.

73 Until January 1986 the official regulations for body searches (taken from Halsbury's *Law of England*) were: "That there was no general common law right to search a person who has been arrested, but such a person may be searched if (i) there are reasonable grounds to suspect that he has on his person any weapon which might do himself or others an injury of any implement which he might use to effect an escape, or (ii) that he has in his possession an article which is material to the offence with which he is charged."
Over the years, the police' power to strip search has been flagrantly abused as a political weapon to degrade and humiliate so-called 'subversives.' On many occasions prisoners have been subjected to internal body searches without having their bags or clothing examined. A recent *Observer* article (27 June 1986) cited the cases of three Asian women arrested in November 1983 outside the House of Leon Brittan, where they had chained themselves to the railings to protest against a deportation. On arrival at the police station the women were forcibly strip searched in front of male police officers.
With the introduction of the Police and Criminal Evidence Act earlier this year the police's statutory powers to strip search have been extended to cover people termed to be "under reasonable suspicion" and can be used "at the discretion of the duty officer."

74 Lord Scarman, *The Brixton Disorders 10-12 April 1981*, HMSO, 1982. Scarman criticised the police of swamp style policing in Brixton, which he claimed contributed to the rioting and the racist behaviour of certain of the officers. he recommended a series of initiatives to be taken by the Metropolitan Police aimed at improving their relationship with the black community.

75 The internal body search ruptured Steve's back passage. He later underwent two operations for this injury.

76 The two written copies of the registration number were later 'lost.'

Chapter 9 — Fear on the Streets: June-November

77 In the October letter, the police, by referring to 'your client,' are obviously suggesting that it was *the* Steven David Shaw who was arrested on May 13th.

78 Much later in the case, Avon and Somerset officers were to tell Steven that they had looked into the matter and it was simply a mistake. They had, they said, talked to the other Steven David Shaw. Investigators later traced as many of the Steven David Shaws in Manchester as they could, but failed to find one who had been arrested.

79 Steve's examination results are another example of the University adminstration's apparent failure to sympathise with him during this period. He was awarded a 2/2 after some discussion. It seems likely that if he had not had his original thesis material stolen and if he had not been subjected to harassment, the University might have awarded him a better degree.

80 The death threat letter and the burglary at the GLC (later in this section) are both indicators that officers in Manchester were able to liase with people in London.

81 *Leon Brittan's visit to Manchester University Students' Union, 1st March 1985,* Report of the Independent Inquiry panel, commission and published by Manchester City Council, November 1985. The members of the panel were John Platt-Mills QC, Tony Bunyan, Keith Ewing, Tony Jefferson and James Wood. Copies are available from the Manchester Police Monitoring Unit, 89, St. James, Buildings, Oxford Road, Manchester.

82 David Waddington visited Manchester University on November 9th 1985.

Chapter 10 — Fear on the Streets: November-February

83 Manchester City Council was willing to go to some lenghts and expenditure in security arrangements for Steve and Sarah. Free supervised transport was offered, as well as minders. Immediately after the attack on Steven on 2nd February a small Defence Committee of lawyers and friends was set up to look after his safety.

84 Some members of the Inquiry panel continued to counsel and support Steve and Sarah long after their task was officially over. Continuing support was also provided by Manchester City Council. Meanwhile, members of the University administration were heard to suggest that as Steven Shaw was no longer a student, he could not be the responsibility of the University.

85

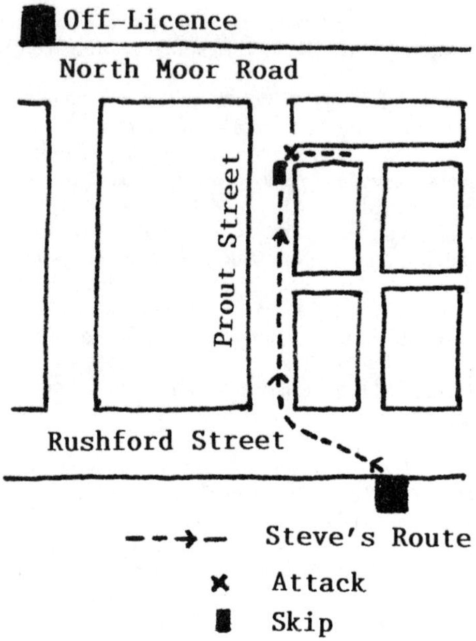

86

MAP II

Chapter 11 — Hunting Ghosts

87 A full page report appeared in the *Guardian* on 24th March 1986. On the same day Steve gave a press conference at the House of Commons. There was also a debate on the matter of the asssaults and harassment of Sarah and Steve on 27th March 1986. (See Hansard Volume 94, No. 87).

Chapter 12 — The Victim Reborn

88 The body of 78 year old Hilda Murrell was found in a remote Shropshire beauty spot a few miles away from her home. The cottage where she had lived

had been ransacked but nothing of any value taken. At the time of her death, Hilda Murrell, an anti-nuclear activist, had been preparing information for the Sizewell B Public Inquiry. Her nephew, a member of the British Navy at the time the Belgrano was sunk, claimed that his aunt had been murdered by the Security Services because of certain confidential information she held about the Sizewell reactor. MP Tam Dalyell claimed that the officers that searched her house were from British Intelligence. See G. Smith's book, *The Death of a Rose Grower,* Cecil Woolf Publications, 1985.

89 Gerald Kaufman, the Shadow Home Secretary and MP for Longsight, the area in which Steven Shaw's second attack took place, has failed to support the campaign to uncover the source of the harassment. At a fringe meeting of the Police Federation Conference in Scarborough in May 1986, Kaufman concurred with police opinion that "Policewatch", produced by the Manchester City Council Police Monitoring Unit was a "scandalous, scurilous, unbalanced and untruthful publication". He also stated that the views contained in the publication were "in no way representative of the Labour leadership."

90 During Ken Livingstone's term of office, the Greater London Council did make progress in this area. As well as encouraging the more structured and official Police Committees, they provided local communities, which set up monitoring groups, with funding and expertise. Unlike the police, the GLC and many Labour London Boroughs were not afraid to help groups which might be critical of their policies. These monitoring groups, staffed by grass roots activists rather than token 'community representatives' were, and still need to be, an essential part of any structure to keep the police in check.

OTHER BOOKS FROM CANARY PRESS

STATE OF SIEGE

Jim Coulter, Susan Miller and Martin Walker

State of Siege documets and analyses the role of the police in the first six months of the 1984-85 miners' strike. Based on first hand interviews and research it is not only acknowledged as one of the most important books on the strike, but represents the first serious look at what are dangerous political developments with a much wider implication.

£3.50 240 pages November 1984

A TURN OF THE SCREW

Martin Walker

A Turn of the Screw is the story of an unfinished struggle. Following the year long 1984-85 miners' strike, a wave of repression swept over the coalfields. Less overt than that experienced during the dispute, this repression was economic, cultural and legal, harder to identlify than the violence handed out by the police on the picket lines. It was met with a series of short strikes as the miners continued to fight back. The strike ended with seven hundred men sacked, over sixty in prison and those back at work harassed by management and in some areas a breakaway union. A Turn of the Screw tells the story in the miners' own words, with analysis and short pieces of fiction. Most importantly the book describes the new consciousness developing among those who were victims of state violence, sackings and imprisonment.

£3.95 132 pages October 1985

SHIFTING HORIZONS

Lynn Beaton

Shifting Horizons describes the part played by two Nottinghamshire miners' wives in the 1984-85 strike. Both women were born and grew up in mining communities and during the strike they fought not just for their future but to preserve their history as well. But as they were to find out, this history had not prepared them for the struggle which was pressed upon them. Forced by events into a new awareness and identity, they found new roles as organisers and activists. Shifting Horizons charts a political journey of two working class women through Thatcher's Britain, two women who fought amongst thousands more for their communities and their dignity. A story of courage and fortitude, of resilience and learning, it is at times touching and filled with raw humour, at other times chilling and painful. It is the story of everywoman in struggle.

£5.65 265 pages October 1985

LET THEM EAT COAL

The Political Use of Social Security During the Miners' Strike

Lesley Sutcliffe and Brian Hill

Let Them Eat Coal explains the political and legislative background to the Thatcher government's policies on welfare benefits. It centres upon the treatment which striking miners in the 1984-85 strike received at the hands of the DHSS and is based upon information received from welfare rights workers throughout the country, together with first hand accounts and interviews with striking miners and their families. The booklet explains the political use of the benefits system by the Conservative government to break the National Union of Mineworkers and starve the strikers and their families back to work.

£1.95 55 pages February 1985

STRIKE BREAKING IN ESSEX

Moira Abdel-Rahim

Strike Breaking in Essex reports on the policing of the miners' picket lines at the Essex ports for the six months form the beginning of April to the end of September 1984. It also includes an examination of the Dartford Tunnel incident, roadblocks and other illegal police activity, the operation of the police 'mutual aid' scheme and an assessment of the cost of the operation. Based on interviews and first hand experience of the picket lines, it exposes not only the role of the police but the attitude of the Essex Police Authority and the view of the Chief Constables during a ruthless campaign to deny picketing rights, crush the miners and step up police powers.

£2.50 121 pages 1985

DEATH IN THE CITY

Melissa Ben and Ken Worpole

Death in the City is an examination of police-related deaths in London. Between 1970 and 1985 over 300 people died in London police stations or in other circumstances related to police activity. Towards the end of the 1970's the numbers rose dramatically. Based upon the personal experience of families and friends, and evidence given at inquests, the book documents some of these deaths and describes the struggle of individuals and communities who set out to find how they occured. What emerges is a catalogue of official indifference, neglect, institutional racism and sexism, human folly and legal maladministration. The book also identifies pointers to the incresing number of deaths in the growing powers of the police, their tactics and their organisation.

£3.95 122 pages January 1986

HEARTS AND MINDS

Joan Witham

Hearts and Minds tells the story of the women of Nottinghamshire in the 1984-1985 Miners' Strike. With the help of interviews, photographs and written material from the strike period, it documents their feelings, their activities and their changing consciousness. Not only did the strikers and their families in Nottinghamshire share the hardship experienced by strikers in other areas, they also suffered some of the worst police brutality of the dispute and the overt hostility of their own friends, families and communities. Yet they are often forgotten amongst the mass of their colleagues who were instrumental in defeating the NUM. This book sets the record straight, in particular on behalf of the women, who struggled against massive odds for their rights, their communities and their self-respect.

£4.95 241 pages September 1986

Available from all good bookshops or by mail order from:
Canary Press
BCM Canary
London WC1N 3XX